'I greatly enjoyed spending time with John Suchet's fascinating book about Johann Strauss, and I hope you will enjoy it as much as I did.'

—André Rieu

'John beautifully balances the family Strauss saga with the fall of the Habsburg Empire . . . terrific!'

—Carl Davis, composer and conductor

'Very readable . . . makes a fascinating read about one of the greatest musical dynasties that ever lived. John Suchet puts their personal lives into the context of the politics of the day without missing out on the musical history. A book to be thoroughly recommended.'

—John Diamond, Chairman of The Johann Strauss Society of Great Britain

'Riveting reading . . . I found it difficult to put down. Stuffed full of facts, both historical and musical, this is in no way a dry academic tome because John Suchet, as always, spins his enthusiastic way through the drama as if guiding us personally in the footsteps of the protagonists and their times. I can highly recommend this absorbing book.'

—Howard Shelley, pianist and conductor

'Engaging . . . the narrative style is very beguiling and draws the reader in very quickly. I could not put this down once I had started it . . . immensely readable, entertaining and beautifully written . . . I loved it.'

—Random Jottings blog

'Incredibly informative and entertaining . . . made me realise how little I knew about this musical dynasty. [Suchet's] talent for giving the reader facts without any heavy academic approach means this is a very approachable route into becoming your own Strauss authority! The snippets and anecdotes have been carefully collected and put together in such a way that dipping in and out of the book is easy – highly recommended for anyone wondering what is behind the Blue Danube!'

—Sandra Parr, Artistic Planning Director (Orchestra and Ensembles), Royal Liverpool Philharmonic Orchestra

CLASSIC *f*M

THE LAST WALTZ

THE STRAUSS DYNASTY
AND VIENNA

JOHN SUCHET

For Nula

First published 2015 by
Elliott and Thompson Limited
27 John Street, London WC1N 2BX
www.eandtbooks.com

This paperback edition published in 2017

ISBN: 978-1-78396-325-6

The author and publishers are grateful to Peter Kemp for permission to reproduce translated quotations that first appeared in *The Strauss Family: Portrait of a Musical Dynasty* (1985). Translations by Robert Nicholls and Peter Eustace.

Picture credits:
Jacket: (Johann Strauss) Hulton-Deutsch / Getty Images, (background) Shutterstock; Page 1: (bottom) DEA/G. DAGLI ORTA/Getty Images; Page 2: (top) Imagno / Getty Images; Page 3: Imagno / Getty Images; Page 4: De Agostini / Getty Images; Page 5: DEA/G. DAGLI ORTA/Getty Images; Page 6: (top) Imagno / Getty Images; Page 7: Imagno / Getty Images; Page 8: (top) DEA/G. DAGLI ORTA/Getty Images, (bottom) iStockPhoto.com.

9 8 7 6 5 4 3 2 1

A catalogue record for this book is available from the British Library.

Printed by by CPI Group (UK) Ltd, Croydon, CR0 4YY

global

Contents

Introduction

The name of Johann Strauss, and the sound of his music, are synonymous with Vienna. They are Vienna. Johann Strauss the Younger, the Waltz King, may have been dead for over a century, but there is not a night of the week when his music cannot be heard somewhere in Vienna. And wherever in the world it is heard, it is the image of the city of Vienna and of its river the Danube that are instantly conjured up.

So beautiful, melodious and instantly memorable are the pieces he wrote, that you could easily believe that he, his father and brothers – prolific and successful composers all – lived in perfect harmony, both musically and other-wise, and that the city of their birth was as peaceful and content as their music.

The truth was very different. The Strauss family was riven with tension, rivalry and jealousy. The founder of the dynasty, Johann Strauss senior, deserted his family. His three sons worked literally to the point of exhaustion – one killing himself through overwork, another constantly ill with the strain of composing, the third ultimately burning thousands of family manuscripts in a fit of jealousy.

And the Vienna in which they lived? A revolution on the streets brought to the throne an emperor who would lose his only son to suicide and his wife to murder. In the second half of the nineteenth century the once great Habsburg Empire would dwindle in power and influence, dwarfed by the might and militarism of Prussia.

Through it all the Viennese would drink champagne and waltz to the music of the Strauss dynasty, as they hurtled towards the First World War and oblivion.

This book tells the extraordinary story of the most prolific and popular family of composers in musical history, and of the turbulent city in which they lived.

Note on Sources:
The principal source of quoted historical material, as well as many other facts pertaining to the lives of the Strauss family, is Peter Kemp's excellent book The Strauss Family: Portrait of a Musical Dynasty. *First published in 1985 and still the most comprehensive and authoritative single-volume work on the Strauss family, this book has been an invaluable help in the researching and writing of* The Last Waltz. *I cannot recommend it highly enough as the starting point for anyone wishing to learn more about this extraordinary family.*

Chapter 1

City of Dreams

There is a saying in Vienna: 'When one eye cries, the other one laughs.' Another has it that 'Things are desperate but not serious.'

Vienna is a city of contradictions, as the Viennese themselves know well, and you need look no further than its music to prove it.

The single most famous piece of music to emerge from Vienna, a piece that encapsulates the spirit of the city, that is heard without fail at every Vienna New Year's Day concert, that from the opening of shimmering violins says 'This is Vienna', is named for its river.

I can think of no other great capital city that has a universally known and loved piece of music named for its river. Not the Seine in Paris, the Thames in London, the

Tiber in Rome, the Vltava in Prague,[*] the Spree in Berlin, the Vistula in Warsaw, the Moskva in Moscow.

But Vienna has '*By the Beautiful Blue Danube*'. And yet every river I have named runs through the centre of its city, *except* the Danube. The Danube skirts round the city of Vienna. For many hundreds of years the traveller arriving by boat in Vienna had quite an onward journey to reach the centre of the city. It was true when Johann Strauss wrote his famous waltz, and it is true today.

How then did this great city come to be indelibly identified with its river through music, a \river that does not even touch it? Just one of the many contradictions of Vienna.

For the explanation behind its wealth of contradictions, take a look at a map of mainland Europe. Vienna sits pretty much at the centre of the landmass. From the earliest times travellers passed through Vienna, from the north, south, east and west, bringing with them their language, customs, ideas and sounds. Inevitably many never left.

During the whole of the nineteenth century, fewer than half of those living in Vienna were Viennese by birth. Not many years before Johann Strauss II was born in 1825, a visitor to Vienna wrote:

> *A feast for the eyes here is the variety of national costumes from different countries … Here you can meet*

---

[*] Perhaps the closest, though 'Vltava' is the second of six symphonic poems which make up Smetana's *Ma Vlast* ('My Homeland').

the Hungarian striding swiftly with his close-fitting
trousers reaching almost to his ankles and his long
pigtail, or the round-headed Pole with his monkish
haircut and flowing sleeves ... Armenians, Romanians
and Moldavians with their half-Oriental costumes ...
Serbians with their twisted moustaches occupy a whole
street – The Greeks in their wide heavy dress can be
seen in hordes smoking their long-stemmed pipes in
the coffee houses ... Bearded Muslims in yellow mules
with their broad murderous knives in their belts ...
Polish Jews all swathed in black, their faces beard-
ed and their hair all twisted in knots ... Bohemian
peasants with their long boots ... Hungarian and
Transylvanian wagoners with sheepskin greatcoats,
Croats with black tubs balanced on their heads – they
all provide entertaining accents in the general throng.

The same visitor wrote that the native languages ('native'
not 'foreign'!) of the Austrian empire were German, Latin,
French, Italian, Hungarian, Bohemian, Polish, Flemish,
Greek, Turkish, Illyrian, Croatian, Slavic, Romanian and
Romany.

Of all the customs and exotica travellers brought with
them, none embedded itself more in the culture – the very
fabric – of Vienna than music.

Here bassoonists and clarinettists are as plentiful as
blackberries ... no place of refreshment, from the

*highest to the lowest, is without music ... one cannot
enter any fashionable house without hearing a duet,
or trio, or finale from one of the Italian operas cur-
rently the rage ... even shopkeepers and cellar-hands
whistle arias.*

Why might this be? First, and most obviously, because of
all the arts music is the most accessible and influential.
Foreigners have long played their music in the streets of
Vienna, and the Viennese have listened enthralled.* But
there is another, more sinister, reason.

In the dying decade of the eighteenth century, Vienna – capital of the Holy Roman Empire, seat of the Holy
Roman Emperor, head of the mighty House of Habsburg
– was a city living in an atmosphere of increasing fear and
suspicion. Just a few hundred miles to the north-west, a
rampaging mob had brought down the French monarchy,
leading first the king, then his queen, to the scaffold, and
was now in the process of trying to obliterate an entire
social class.

No other city in Continental Europe was as class
conscious, as socially structured, as Vienna, and no other
monarchy as powerful or autocratic as the Habsburgs. If
the British monarchy – and people – had at least a narrow
but forbiddingly protective stretch of water to safeguard

---

* It happens to this day. On my last visit to Vienna, just a couple of
years ago, I stood in a crowd listening to street musicians playing folk
music from the Andes.

them, then Vienna, its monarchy and its aristocracy, were obvious first targets if the new French rulers decided to export their revolution by means of the French Revolutionary Army under their brilliant young commander Napoleon Bonaparte.

Austria's iron-willed chancellor, Klemens von Metternich, had the answer. He simply brought the shutters down on Europe's most vibrant city. A network of spies was created; any activity remotely seditious was immediately reported; people of all classes thought before they spoke, and when they did speak they took great care over what they said. Anything else was simply too dangerous.

Which, in a nutshell, is how Vienna came to be Europe's capital city of music. If words are not safe, what is? Music. Who can say that a folk band in a tavern, a café, or on a street corner, is fomenting dissent? And so Europe's musicians flocked to Vienna. A roll-call of composers who lived or worked in Vienna, or merely visited it in the century and a half to 1900, is like a recitation of some of the greatest names in music: Haydn, Mozart, Beethoven, Schubert, Mendelssohn, Schumann, Wagner, Johann Strauss II, Bruckner, Brahms, Mahler – and they are only the best known.

Yet, of those great names, only two were actually Viennese, born in Vienna. Franz Schubert and Johann Strauss. And of these two, one alone can be said to encapsulate Vienna in his music – the zest, sounds, rhythms, excitement, laughter, gaiety and sadness.

5

The music of Johann Strauss does not just encapsulate the contradictions of Vienna; it provides an explanation for them and in so doing it supersedes them. The most famous couplet of his best-loved operetta, *Die Fledermaus*, reads: 'Happy is he who is able to forget what he cannot change.'* A more succinct summation of the Viennese character – and indeed for those Viennese not naturally blessed with it one they were able to adopt – is hard to find. To think of Johann Strauss, to listen to his music, is to think of Vienna and hear its sounds.

But it was a long and dangerous journey from the carefree days described by that earlier traveller to the era of Strauss, the waltz and champagne. In between came nearly four decades of fear and tension.

Vienna has always been something of a frontier city. In Metternich's time it was a pointed joke to say that on the other side of the city's most easterly tollgate the Orient began. A century and a half later Vienna was the last city in the West before the barbed wire and sentry posts marked the beginning of communist Eastern Europe. Buildings that once looked out over the Hungarian plain, from where the Ottoman army came to besiege Vienna, now looked out over a land whose people were shut off from the West on pain of death.†

---

* 'Glücklich ist wer vergisst, was doch nicht zu ändern ist.'
† The 1949 film *The Third Man* perfectly portrays Vienna, the frontier city.

Vienna, then, has been well acquainted with danger and intrigue. The decades between the Congress of Vienna in 1814, which attempted to redraw the post-Napoleonic map of Europe, and the revolutions of 1848 that swept away the old order, were to stamp themselves indelibly on the Viennese character. During those long years the city, and its people, turned in on themselves.

The period is known to us as the Biedermeier era, and it introduced a particular word to the lexicon: '*Gemütlichkeit*', a word that cannot be translated into a single English equivalent. It is a state of mind that is cheerful, happy and unworried, accepting of what life may bring.

A close approximation of the meaning of '*Gemütlichkeit*' in English would be a sort of comfortableness, cosiness, even amiability. Yet how could such a mood exist in a city of fear? The answer is simple. It existed in the comfort of your own home – and only there.

That is where the name 'Biedermeier' comes in. It derived originally from a series of humorous poems depicting a comically naive schoolteacher by the name of Papa Biedermeier. By a series of mutations, the name came to describe the comfort and safety of your own home in a city where talk in a public place was dangerous.

In those tense years the Viennese simply stayed at home, where they knew they would be safe, or visited the homes of close friends and associates. Aristocrats, patrons of the arts, held soirées in their palaces. For the upper classes it was a salon life replete with culture.

To a degree this was simply an extension of how it had always been. A generation earlier the young Beethoven had made his name in the salons of the nobility, who were stunned at his extraordinary virtuosity and his ability to improvise on the piano. Franz Schubert entertained friends at home with such regularity that the evenings were known as Schubertiades.

Then, in 1825, Johann Strauss the Younger was born – right in the middle of the Biedermeier era, he grew up under its influence. His music is inseparable from the period.

So how does the Strauss dynasty fit into this rich and complex tapestry? How did the music of a father and his three sons come to encapsulate the spirit of that contradictory city so perfectly?

On 14 March 1804 a child born in a small tavern on the banks of the Danube in the run-down Viennese suburb of Leopoldstadt was given the name Johann. His father, who managed the tavern, was Franz Strauss. Thanks to this child the name Strauss would forever be linked to music and the Viennese waltz.

It was a propitious time for a musician to be born. The Irish tenor Michael Kelly, visiting Vienna twenty years earlier, where he befriended Mozart, spoke of a city where it seemed the whole populace danced. There were dance halls in all the suburbs, and most taverns had a resident band and a space for dancing.

Taking their cue from the victorious revolutionaries in Paris, the stately dances that had been the province of the aristocracy – the minuet, the allemande, the bourrée – were quickly replaced by the stamping and whirling dances that had been familiar in village taverns across southern Germany for generations, the '*Ländler*'.*

With increasing boat travel east along the Danube, across Bavaria and into Austria, it was not long before the bucolic rhythms and sounds reached Europe's most sophisticated city, Vienna. They were soon taken up by resident bands in the city's dance halls and taverns, and the common populace delighted in the new entertainment, beer mugs overflowing, feet stamping.

There was a unique feature that set these dances apart from the dances of the nobility. The man and woman faced each other, arms entwined, bodies clasped tightly. In other words they danced as a couple, as opposed to dancing partners facing mostly in the same direction, their hands possibly touching lightly in the air.

In the wake of the French Revolution there was a new feeling of freedom and release among the lower social classes in aristocratic Vienna. It would not last, of course, once Metternich took matters in hand, but in the closing decade of the eighteenth century and the opening decade of the

---

* 'Of the country', or 'rural'.

nineteenth, for the first time music, fashion and tastes in general permeated up the social scale rather than down.

They did not survive the transition entirely intact, however. The polished wooden floors of aristocratic salons, so suited to the leather-soled shoes of the aristocracy, might have been the perfect surface on which to dance the minuet, but they were entirely unsuited to the *Ländler* and the boots and clogs in which they were normally danced.

And so, over a remarkably short period of time, the stomp developed into a slide, the hobnail gave way to leather. The new dance was in three-four time, the man holding the woman close, one hand clasping hers, the other pressing her body to his. Faces could be close, cheeks could touch, lips brush lightly. The waltz was born.* This was the sound, the rhythm, that young Johann listened to from his earliest years, that he grew up hearing. It was said that as a child he would creep down from his bedroom and hide under tables so he could hear the music and watch the couples dance.

It was as well he had music as a distraction, because his early years were fraught with sadness. When he was just seven years old, his mother died from fever. His father remarried, but five years later his body was found floating in the river that ran swiftly past the tavern he managed. It was never established whether he drowned accidentally or committed suicide.

---

* From the verb '*walzen*', 'to turn'.

Johann's father left a debt-ridden estate and it was no surprise that his stepmother apprenticed the boy months later to a tailor, who very soon passed him on to a book-binder. The boy, now thirteen, hated this apprenticeship, complaining years later that his whole boyhood stank of glue.

But there was salvation. Exactly how Johann Strauss came into possession of a cheap Bavarian violin made of poor-quality wood is not known. It is possible his new stepfather – by all accounts a kindly man – gave it to him. It is just as likely it was abandoned by an itinerant musician after a night's drinking. What is certain, however, is that it swiftly became the boy's most treasured possession.[*]

He took to it like a duck to water. We know he received violin lessons, though not from whom, and this preoccupation with music ran alongside his bookbinding apprenticeship. At the age of just fifteen, possibly even younger, he landed a place in the highly popular dance orchestra led by violinist and conductor Michael Pamer. This impressed his stepfather enough to allow him to leave the smell of glue behind to pursue a career as musician.[†]

Pamer was an interesting character. Forced to give up the violin because of an injury to his left index finger, he

---

[*] I would like to believe the story that when the tone of the fiddle was too dry and thin, Johann would pour beer into it to give a more moist, and consequently sentimental, tone.

[†] It's possible he actually played viola in the orchestra, which would be even more impressive.

made up for it with monumental intakes of beer – while conducting. Pamer's showpiece was a number to which he gave the nickname '*Blessed Memories of Hütteldorf Beer*', pausing to drink a mugful in honour of the memory after each piece. The audience, entering into the game, regularly called for as many as twenty encores, resulting in Pamer collapsing in a heap in front of the orchestra and conducting on his back.

It is surely not too fanciful to imagine a young and impressionable Johann Strauss, sitting in the orchestra and observing closely how extroversion and showmanship can involve an audience more closely in music making, even if this particular example was somewhat extreme.

There was another young member of the violin section in Pamer's orchestra, three years older than Johann, by the name of Joseph Lanner. The two must have formed a friendship, because it was not long before both had resigned from the orchestra and were working together. Lanner had been the first to leave, setting up his own trio with two friends, soon to be joined by Strauss, the trio becoming a quartet. Johann and Joseph formed a close bond, even sharing lodgings.

These two highly talented violinists soon attracted attention, not least because they were such opposites. 'Black Schani' (Strauss) was olive-skinned with dark wavy hair, described by the Viennese in local dialect as 'peppery', 'vibrant', even 'sharp-tongued'. 'Blond Peppi' (Lanner) by contrast was 'mild', 'smooth', 'silken'.

That applied to their music too, because what set these two apart from the many other musicians playing in orchestras and bands was that both began to compose. Lanner, as the older and more experienced, was the more productive of the two. Although – in an uncanny prescience of what would happen a generation later to an as yet unborn Johann Strauss the Younger – the strain of rehearsing, conducting, arranging and composing began to take a toll on Lanner's health.

Lanner, the driving force in the partnership, had expanded his quartet to a small string orchestra, and when that proved insufficient to handle the ever increasing workload, formed a second orchestra. He appointed his friend and partner, Johann Strauss, as 'vice-conductor' of this orchestra.

It proved to be a mistake – for Lanner. The young Johann Strauss, just turned twenty-one, had found his calling. Suddenly his boundless energy, his hitherto untapped organisational skills, his natural authority, the ability to lead, set him apart. Once Lanner asked him to come up swiftly with a set of waltzes for an event that same evening – he was too unwell to do it himself. Just once and never again. It was a triumph for Strauss.

There was no holding him. He did more than just compose. He arranged pieces by other composers, hired the musicians, and booked venues. But what impressed the ever growing audiences most of all was that Johann Strauss led the orchestra from the violin. This was not unknown in Vienna, or in taverns along the Danube. But usually the violinist would stand in front of a small handful of musicians, his part no more or less important than theirs. Strauss did more than just play or accompany. He led. No one doubted who was in charge, or who took the bows at the end.

The young man developed a certain swagger, as his name began to be talked of around town. It was not long before Strauss realised he had the skills, and the public recognition, to forge a career on his own. The friend and colleague who had given him his break was now superfluous, if not actually a hindrance. He went to Lanner and told him he planned a solo career. Lanner knew full well what he was losing and the discussions, which took place over a number of days, became increasingly heated. Matters reached a head at a concert the two men gave together at a large ballroom by the name of Zum Bock ('At the Ram').

In the early hours of the morning, with the concert over and large quantities of alcohol consumed, the two men – so legend has it – came to blows. Instruments were damaged and furniture was smashed. There was no going back. It was a parting of the ways, which Lanner commemorated in his '*Trennungswalzer*' ('Separation Waltz').*

Johann Strauss was on his own. Well, not entirely. In

---

* There is no documentary evidence of the fracas, but why should there be? Certainly it was the talk of Vienna within a very short time, and even if an element of exaggeration has crept in, there is no doubt the two young men parted acrimoniously.

the first place he took fourteen of Lanner's best musicians with him, which allowed him to put together a serviceable orchestra from the start. Secondly, and of considerably more importance to musical history, he had met a young woman and fallen in love.

Anna Streim was the daughter of the landlord of Zum roten Hahn ('At the Red Rooster'), a tavern in a suburb of Vienna. Johann wooed and won Anna, and on 11 July 1825 the couple were married. Johann was twenty-one, his bride two years older. Less than four months later, on 25 October 1825, Anna gave birth. The baby was a boy, and he was named after his father. This was the Johann Strauss who would go on to eclipse his father as a musician, and become the best-loved, most prolific, internationally lauded composer that the city of Vienna had ever – or would ever – produce.

Chapter 2

Café Culture

If Vienna was Europe's capital city of music, it was also – and still is – the European capital of the café. It is possible there was a café in Oxford, or Venice, earlier than in Vienna, but it was in the Habsburg capital that the café or coffee house firmly took root and became a way of life. The reason for this is not hard to find. The Habsburg empire traded closely with the Ottoman empire, and the coffee bean so prevalent in Istanbul quickly made its way to Vienna, where it was in abundant supply. Cafés soon proliferated in the city and became the favoured places to meet, gossip and listen to local bands.

But there is a much more interesting and engaging explanation of how Vienna came to be the café capital of Europe, and it is one known to the Viennese today, and certainly to most Viennese of earlier centuries, in particular to musicians for whom the café, and later the dance hall, were to provide so many new venues for their work. It is, of course, a legend, and as such has become embroidered over the passage of time, but a legend becomes so only because it is based on truth, and this one has more than a ring of truth about it.

Every legend has a hero, and the name of this one is Georg Franz Kolschitzky.* A Polish street trader, Kolschitzky had spent some years travelling and trading in Turkey and so became fluent in Turkish and familiar with Turkish customs and traditions. At one time he had served as translator in the Turkish army. He was therefore the right man in the right place when the Turks, for the second time in a century and a half, sent a huge army west with the aim of conquering Europe and destroying Christendom. The Crusades in reverse, as it were. After the first failed attempt under Suleiman the Magnificent, when the siege was broken by the Viennese, a massive defensive wall – the Bastei – had been built around the city with the explicit aim of keeping out any later attempt.

Now, in 1683, that wall threatened to prove more of a hindrance than a help. An army of 300,000 Turks simply set up camp outside it, prevented any movement of supplies through its ten gates, and waited for the Viennese, holed up inside, to surrender before they starved. The Glacis, the expanse of green that lay beyond the wall, bristled with tents, and the air was filled with smoke and the exotic aromas of Levantine spices.

---

* Variously Kolschitzky, Koltschitzki, Kulczycki.

The commander of the meagre forces inside the city wall, Count Starhemberg, was aware that help, of a kind, was at hand. The Duke of Lorraine was camped on the other side of the Danube with a force of just 33,000 men – no match for the Turks. But King Jan Sobieski of Poland had left Warsaw and was gathering forces as he marched southwest to Vienna. If and when Sobieski and Lorraine could join forces, there was the faint hope that the Turks could be defeated and the siege lifted.

The situation inside the city wall was becoming desperate. Starhemberg knew time was short and it was imperative to get word out to Lorraine of just how serious things were, and how quickly help was needed. Several times he dispatched envoys with orders to get through enemy lines, only to see their bodies hanging outside the city wall days later as a warning and deterrent.

Enter the man who could speak fluent Turkish, understood Turkish ways, and could – with a measure of good fortune – pass himself off as one of the enemy. Could Kolschitzky succeed where others had failed?

On 13 August he left the city and walked through the Turkish encampment, passing himself off as a trader from Belgrade. So successful was he that at one point he was captured by locals in the little village of Kahlenberg and only managed to persuade them he was not one of the enemy by speaking to them in a Viennese dialect no one who was not Viennese could possibly know.

Kolschitzky reached Lorraine safely. A rocket was fired

off to signify this, and a rocket was fired from the roof of St Stephen's Cathedral in the city in acknowledgement. Kolschitzky apprised Lorraine of the dire situation inside the city wall and the desperate need for action. Lorraine dispatched couriers to Sobieski and other European leaders, urging them to send forces to Vienna at maximum speed, warning that otherwise Vienna would be lost, leaving Europe at the mercy of the Muslim horde.

His task complete, Kolschitzky made the dangerous return journey to the besieged city. He came even closer to having his cover blown on this return trip, he later said, and had to call on every ounce of skill and deception that he possessed. Against all the odds he arrived safely back in Vienna on 17 August.

Less than a month later a large relief force made up of Poles, Germans, Austrians and several other European nationalities gathered on the summit of Mount Kahlenberg, at the extreme eastern end of the Vienna woods, overlooking the city. At midnight on 11 September the troops were blessed in an outdoor mass, and at dawn on the 12th, led by the Polish king, they charged down the hillside straight into the Turkish camp.

A defensive line of Turkish trenches to the north-west of the city was quickly overwhelmed,* and after a fierce but one-sided battle the Turks were routed. They fled in

---

* On the site today stands a large park called the Türkenschanzpark, 'Turkish trench park'.

disarray, unable even to dismantle their tents or pack up goods and equipment. It was the last attempt by a Turkish army to invade Europe.

King Jan Sobieski of Poland became an instant hero across Europe, to this day revered by Poles who will tell you that their king saved Christendom and that had it not been for him Europe would now be Muslim. Kolschitzky became an instant hero in Vienna and a grateful Emperor Leopold asked him to choose a reward from the bounty the Turks had left behind.

And what exactly had the Turks left behind? The inventory included 25,000 tents, 10,000 oxen, 5,000 camels, 100,000 bushels of grain, a huge quantity of gold, and hundreds of sacks filled with green beans that no one in Vienna had seen before or knew what use to make of them. No one except Kolschitzky, who from his time in Istanbul knew instantly that they were coffee beans. He asked the emperor for the sacks and their contents, and permission to open an establishment serving the drink he would make from the beans, known as coffee. The emperor was only too pleased to oblige.

Thus Vienna acquired its first coffee house, or café, and the Viennese first fell in love with the drink that would come to epitomise them. Well, not quite that easily. For, as the legend goes, the drink that Kolschitzky first brewed was much too bitter for Viennese tastes and it failed to catch on.

Then someone suggested to Kolschitzky that he should add milk. This improved matters considerably, but still he failed to make a success of the venture. Another suggestion: why don't you use cream instead of milk, and whip it?

The rest, as they say, is history. Now it might well be that these last few details have accrued something in the telling, but the fact remains that to this day there is a street in Vienna named after Georg Franz Kolschitzky, the Kolschitzkygasse, and on the corner of it, on the first floor, is a statue of Kolschitzky in Turkish garb, holding a tray with coffee cups, erected by a grateful Coffee Makers Guild of Vienna.

To say that Kolschitzky started something is an understatement. Cafés proliferated across the city. By the 1830s there were eighty coffee houses in the city centre, and at least fifty more in the suburbs. This coincided with an equally extensive proliferation of dance halls in Vienna. As a new century dawned there were the beginnings of mechanical industry that within a few decades would revolutionise people's lives. There was more wealth than ever before, and with it the Viennese demanded more entertainment, more opportunity for relaxation.

That meant music, and music meant dancing. Coffee houses became ever more numerous, and dance halls – taking their cue from Paris – became more and more luxurious. Elaborate chandeliers hung from the ceiling, a thousand wax candles glittering in them. In the centre of one hall, the Apollo Palace, sat an immense rock from which springs flowed out in tumbling cascades, down into large tanks filled with live fish.

But the most sensational import from the French capital was wooden parquet flooring, never before seen in Vienna. What could be better for the new dance that was swiftly becoming a craze? The waltz was taking hold in Vienna at just the time the young Johann Strauss I was weighing up the possibilities of a solo career. The style and rhythms of the music came naturally to him. He played it and he wrote it, and the Viennese delighted in it.

In a remarkable confluence of increased sophistication, public taste, a desire for change, and the move into a new century, the waltz took hold in Vienna, never to leave it. It could not have been a better moment for a certain young musician to strike out on his own, form his own orchestra, experiment with his own compositions, see if he could make a name for himself.

Johann Strauss the Elder was on his way.

But things were not easy. Johann Strauss had a growing family, mouths to feed. A second son, Josef, was born less than two years after Johann junior, followed by two girls, Anna and Therese, again at two-yearly intervals. A fifth child lived only ten months, and in March 1835 the couple's sixth and last child, Eduard, was born. A growing family necessitated more living space and they moved house four times in under ten years, each time to more expensive accommodation.

It meant Johann senior had to work hard, and this he certainly did. Compositions poured from him. By the time of his first real success, the '*Sperls Fest-Walzer*', a piece he composed to celebrate his debut at Vienna's newest and most prestigious dance hall, the Sperl, he had already composed nearly thirty pieces, not just waltzes but gallops as well.

As his fame grew, musicians clamoured to work with him, and he was impressing some rather big names in the world of music. Writing with characteristic hyperbole, a certain Richard Wagner, who visited Vienna in the summer of 1832, said:

> *I shall never forget the extraordinary playing of Johann Strauss, who ... made the audience almost frantic with delight. At the beginning of a new waltz this demon of the Viennese musical spirit shook like a Pythian princess on the tripod, and veritable groans of ecstasy which, without doubt, were more due to his music than to the drinks in which the audience had indulged, raised their worship for the magic violinist to almost bewildering heights of frenzy.*

Strauss had learned well from the flamboyance of Michael Pamer. Frédéric Chopin too, then only twenty-one, noted a year earlier that 'Lanner, Strauss and their waltzes obscure everything'.

But Johann Strauss was soon to leave Lanner far behind, as word of the magic that this remarkable young musician seemed to instil in audiences, and the flamboyance with which he led his orchestra from the violin – 'His own limbs no longer belong to him when the desert storm of his waltz is let loose, his fiddle bow dances with his arms, the melody waves champagne glasses in his face,' wrote one reveller after an evening at the Sperl – spread beyond his home city of Vienna.

It was not long before Johann Strauss and his orchestra took to the road. A short trip down the Danube led to a sparkling performance in Pest – 'Herr Strauss triumphed … with the first stroke of his bow' – and after several more months of concerts and balls in Vienna, Strauss received an extraordinary invitation to travel with his orchestra to Berlin.

Berlin, capital of Prussia, formal, correct, proper, militaristic, as far removed from the easy-going culture of Vienna several hundred miles to the south as it was possible to be. But this was no ordinary invitation. Strauss found himself performing before the King of Prussia at his court, and his highly distinguished guests the Tsar and Empress of Russia.

So enthralled were the royal personages that the king rewarded Strauss handsomely with a fee so large it was packed in a satchel, and the tsar presented him with a golden snuffbox. A normally sober-minded and restrained Berlin newspaper critic wrote, 'Look at little Strauss. He has turned all our good citizens into Viennese.' Another was so overwhelmed that he seemed to lose control of his critical faculties:

I am so happy, so joyful, so glad that I want to kiss the heavens with their stars; so recklessly, deliriously happy that I want to embrace the whole world and press it to my heart! And why? Because I have heard him! I have heard Johann Strauss!

On the return journey to Vienna, Strauss and his orchestra performed in Leipzig, Dresden and Prague. Months later they left on another tour – a three-month trip through southern Germany, performing forty concerts in nineteen different towns. The following year saw their most extensive and ambitious tour to date. It lasted almost four months and took them back to Prague and Leipzig, then to Hanover and Hamburg, from there to Amsterdam, Rotterdam, Düsseldorf, Cologne and Brussels, and finally back to Vienna to arrive the day before New Year's Eve, 1835.

Everywhere the orchestra played the audience seemed to relish a feeling of liberation, as if they had at last been given permission to get up and dance, to smile and laugh, sing and shout, drink and dance their troubles away. Johann Strauss had struck a chord, literally.

As well as the unique sight – certainly outside Vienna – of seeing Strauss leading from the violin, swaying in time to the music, his waving bow a thousand times more expressive than a conductor's baton, there was something else that set Johann Strauss apart. He would frequently mark a visit to a town or city by composing a new piece in its honour, and performing it before a suitably flattered audience.

For that first visit to Pest, he composed '*Emlek Pestre – Erinnerung an Pesth*' ('Memory of Pest'), and for Berlin '*Erinnerung an Berlin*' ('Memory of Berlin'). By the time he returned to Vienna at the end of 1835 he had composed more than eighty pieces; more than eighty opus numbers to his name. Vienna had not seen anything like it. Johann Strauss, barely turned thirty years of age, was a phenomenon.

But his new-found fame was coming at a price. On his return from Pest – and that was before Berlin and the other towns and cities – Strauss wrote to his doctor, 'My left arm is very strained, which I attribute to my playing the violin, which hurts me.' Not a good omen for the future. There was another problem too, and one he could do nothing about. Despite the extraordinary reviews and seemingly ubiquitous adulation, Strauss's music was not meeting with universal approval. In certain sectors of Protestant northern Germany there was open hostility towards the waltz, which was, in the eyes of these strict moralists, an infestation from the Catholic south.

The dance was condemned as 'an incitement to sinful passion', and decried as 'demoralising and lewd'. Protestant zealots recruited the medical profession to their side and published a treatise entitled *Proof That the Waltz is a Main Cause of the Weakness of Body and Mind of Our Generation*.* They could point to actual harm caused by the waltz.

---

* *Beweis, dass der Walzer eine Hauptquelle der Schwäche des Körpers und des Geistes unserer Generation sey.*

Some dancers had fainted due to over-exertion and there had even been reports of deaths. These sad occurrences had affected men more than women, a sure sign – as the opposition were careful to avoid saying – of enjoyment and indulgence taken to extreme.

These were not just a small number of disaffected Protestants preaching to deaf ears. In some towns they succeeded in having their opposition to the waltz enshrined in law on the grounds that it was inimical to health. In others, including cities as important as Magdeburg and Frankfurt, police edicts were issued against the 'improper and horrible turning of women by men', particularly if done in such a manner as 'to make skirts fly up and reveal too much'.

Disaffection with the waltz, though, could not last. It was impossible to withstand the avalanche of popularity and enthusiasm that swept not just Austria and Germany but beyond their borders and across Europe. Johann Strauss and his orchestra were growing more popular internationally by the day, and the name of Johann Strauss was fast becoming the best-loved musical name in Europe. What could possibly go wrong? The answer is a lot. Nothing to do with music. It was much nearer home than that, and it was to have a profound effect on the Strausses of the next generation.

Chapter 3

Conquering Paris

L ife 'on the road' held many attractions for Johann
Strauss I, not least the perfect justification to absent
himself from a naturally disorganised household with five
children ranging, at the end of 1835, from ten years of age
to twelve months.

There were also all the temptations open to a young,
highly attractive man, spending every night away from
home. I have already noted Strauss's unusual complexion,
compared to the typically blond Viennese Joseph Lanner.
Strauss's paternal grandparents were both Jewish, and he
had inherited their dark complexion.[*] He had lustrous
black wavy hair and there are numerous descriptions of

---

[*] This led to one of the most bizarre acts of documentary falsification of
the Third Reich, as it tried to obliterate any trace of Jewish ancestry in a
family that it held up as a perfect example of Aryanism. See chapter 22.

his sparkling eyes, dazzling good looks and magnetic personality.

There was no shortage of female admirers at his concerts, and Strauss was not reluctant to benefit from what was on offer. There is no doubt word got back to Anna in Vienna, and she seems to have accepted his transgressions as a price to be paid for a successful and lucrative career, which had allowed the family to move into a spacious and elegant house in a smart area of the city. That changed, though, when Anna received information that suggested that one liaison had become rather more permanent than the others, that Johann in fact had a mistress, not in some distant town, but in Vienna itself.

Emilie Sophia Anna Trampusch* was, by all accounts, an attractive and charming young woman who worked as a milliner. Ten years younger than Strauss, she lived in a small apartment in Kumpfgasse, close to St Stephen's Cathedral in the centre of the city. The Strausses' house was across the Danube canal in Taborstrasse, which ran alongside the leafy and green Augarten park, a carriage ride of not more than ten or fifteen minutes from St Stephen's.

It is probable the liaison began before Strauss left on that first tour. But what Anna was totally unprepared for was the news that reached her just two months after her youngest child, Eduard, was born. Emilie had borne

---

* Variously Trampusch, Trambusch, Tramposch. The name, in whichever form, is inelegant to Austrian ears and will have been mocked by her detractors.

Strauss an illegitimate daughter, and he was openly and brazenly admitting he was the father.

Far from being repentant, he continued the relationship, and exactly one year and ten days later Emilie gave birth again, this time to a son. He was christened Johann Wilhelm. Anna now had to contend not only with the fact that her husband had a second family, but that the eldest son was named Johann, just as her eldest son was.

It did not end there. Over the following ten years Emilie gave birth six more times. Only three of the eight children survived into adulthood and they were the three eldest, two daughters and a son. All three kept their mother's name, so that there was one Johann Strauss senior and two half-brothers, Johann Strauss junior and Johann Trampusch. None of the three illegitimate Strauss children has earned even a footnote in history. I find it surprising, given that their father was an extraordinarily gifted musician and their mother later became an actress – artistic talent therefore to some extent on both sides – that none of the three possessed any aptitude in music or any other of the arts.* It is perhaps even more surprising that his three legitimate sons all became prolific composers, one of undoubted genius.

Johann Strauss senior had fathered fourteen children with two women in twenty-one years. He had two families

---

* There is some evidence the eldest, Emilie, followed her mother onto the stage, but it is not known with what success.

and ran two households, which was an open secret among musical circles in Vienna. During roughly the same period he had composed the best part of a hundred pieces, and his name was becoming known across Europe, which quite simply had never seen a musician like Johann Strauss. He composed most of the pieces he performed. Broadly they were a mixture of gallops, waltzes and polkas, all designed for dance and amusement. They were not just trifles. It did not take the musically sophisticated Viennese long to realise these were substantial pieces, perfectly calculated to entertain an audience.

There was also his infectious personality. He did more than simply lead from the violin; the music seemed to inhabit his body. Swaying with the violin under his chin one moment, waving it – and the bow – in the air the next, turning to the audience while playing, smiling all the time. And his were not audiences sitting in serried rows of seats, formally attired, speaking only in the quietest of whispers, taking care not to cough. These were dance-hall audiences, eating, drinking, laughing, conversing and, most importantly of all, dancing.

Given his growing reputation it was hardly surprising when an invitation came to travel to the most sophisticated city, artistically speaking, in mainland Europe, where audiences were notoriously critical, even cruel. It would be a challenge, a risk. The Strauss sounds and rhythms might be much loved in central Europe, but how would they go down nearly eight hundred miles to the west, in Paris?

In the late afternoon of 4 October 1837 Johann Strauss and an orchestra of twenty-eight musicians boarded coaches for the overland journey to the French capital. There were several stop-offs on the way for concerts in southern Germany, and then in Strasbourg. They arrived in Paris on 27 October, no doubt exhausted from an arduous journey with performances along the way. The first concert was scheduled for 1 November, giving them just four days to recover, settle in and rehearse.

To add to his anxiety Strauss learned that tickets had been sold at inflated prices, and his nerves were hardly calmed when he was informed that the cream of Parisian musical society would be in the audience. The most recognisable, with his mop of carrot-coloured hair, was also the most revered, Hector Berlioz. Other respected names, if not at this first concert then at subsequent performances, were Meyerbeer, Cherubini, Auber and Adolphe Adam (whose most famous ballet *Giselle* was still four years off).

It was with understandable trepidation therefore that Johann Strauss mounted the podium in front of his orchestra in the Salle des Gymnases. He need not have worried. Using flattery once again as a potent weapon – '*Der Carneval in Paris*' and the '*Paris Walzer*' (which contained a quotation from *La Marseillaise* in waltz-time!) had been specially composed – even this sophisticated Parisian audience could not resist the infectious sounds and rhythms of the Strauss orchestra.

Berlioz himself, considered by many (including himself) to be the natural successor of Beethoven, no less, wrote in the *Journal des Débats*:

> *We knew the name of Strauss, but that was all. Of the fire, the intelligence, and the rhythmic feeling which his orchestra displays, we had no notion … Their waltzes are difficult to play, but how easily the Viennese accomplish it, how they charm us with their piquant rhythmic coquetry!*

Where Berlioz led others followed, and it can have come as no surprise to Strauss that he soon received a formal invitation to perform at the very top – at the Tuileries Palace in the presence of King Louis-Philippe of France.

This was a very different monarchy from the one that had been brutally terminated less than a half-century earlier. Louis-Philippe was a distant relative of the ill-fated Louis XVI and enjoyed a fully aristocratic upbringing, but had some sympathy with the revolutionaries' aims, if not methods, and was keen to portray himself as a man of the people. So successful was he, at least in the early years of his reign, that he earned the sobriquet 'The Bourgeois King'.

Strauss and his men walked along the same corridors that had been stormed and in which the blood of the Swiss

Guard was spilled during the revolution, to be greeted personally by the king, which no doubt surprised Strauss who was more accustomed to the rigid etiquette and formality of Vienna. He was flattered to hear the king say, 'Your waltzes have been familiar to me for a long time, my dear Herr Strauss. It gives me all the more pleasure that you have done me the honour of appearing here personally.'

The success of the performance was a foregone conclusion. Afterwards Louis-Philippe made an impromptu speech of congratulations and thanks to the Viennese musicians, all enjoyed champagne, and the king took both of Strauss's hands in his – all in all, a scenario that would have been unthinkable in the presence of a French monarch not many years before.

If the king represented the highest personage Strauss and his musicians were to meet during their stay in Paris, then unquestionably the single musical figure they were most honoured to meet was an Italian violinist whose name was known across Europe. Now in the autumn of his years, suffering from the syphilis he had contracted many years before and a recent bout of pneumonia, Niccolò Paganini attended one of Strauss's concerts incognito, slipping into the back row unseen.

But the disguise was instantly spotted and he was ushered to the front of the hall and into a place of honour. Strauss came onto the podium, had his attention directed to the famous musician, instantly left the podium and the two men embraced. In a faltering voice, but clear enough for the audience to hear, Paganini said, 'I am glad to meet a man who has brought so much joy to the world.'

Everywhere the orchestra went they were lauded and applauded. Strauss's musicians were aware that they belonged to the most in-demand orchestra in Europe, that they were travelling to towns and cities they could not otherwise have expected to see in a normal lifetime, meeting royalty, aristocrats, composers, fellow musicians. Yet for the first time since Strauss formed his orchestra, there were the beginnings of an undercurrent of malaise. Not too strong, at least not to begin with, but a matter he would sooner or later have to confront.

By February 1838 the musicians had been away from home and family for the best part of five months, including over Christmas. Several of them had written home bemoaning the fact that the French did not take much notice of Christmas – no Christmas trees! – and when they did it was without a proper sense of its religious significance: dancing in the streets when they should have been attending midnight Mass.

There was a growing feeling among the players that it was time to return to Vienna. Strauss was aware of the demands he was making on them, the exhausting journeys by horse-drawn carriage, the busy schedule of concerts – often arranged at the last minute. One player wrote home that they were all enjoying a midday meal nine days before Christmas, when Strauss rushed in and told them to hurry up because they needed to leave for Rouen where they had just been booked to play at a masked ball and give three more concerts.

To head off any complaints about conditions, Strauss had made it a policy to spare no expense when it came to comfort. For the four months of the stay in Paris he took over an entire hotel, and in the particularly harsh Paris winter of 1836–7 he ordered every room to be individually heated. Meals were frequent and abundant, consisting of several courses. All players were paid promptly, and one wrote that several of the men, himself included, had received salary in advance when required. 'Strauss cares for his men just as a fond father cares for his children,' he put it.

But still there were rumblings of discontent, and Strauss knew what no one else in the party knew. There had been a development that was bound to bring matters to a head.

Across the Channel the people of Britain were preparing for what they knew to be imminent: the death of the old king and the accession to the throne of a young princess by the name of Victoria. The coronation would unleash festivities such as the country had not seen for a long time, and the invitation had come to Johann Strauss for his orchestra to be part of it. Not only had he a pocketful of invitations to perform for members of the aristocracy, but he could also expect to play in the presence of the princess, soon to be queen, in Buckingham Palace. This would be the pinnacle for the young Viennese musician and his orchestra. Turning it down was simply not an option.

Strauss's reputation had travelled ahead of him and already there was excitement that this new dance, the waltz, might soon be coming to British shores, with all the opportunities it offered for romance, illicit liaisons and sexual intrigue – none of these pursuits entirely unknown in British aristocratic circles. Sophisticated appetites had been whetted by no less a figure than the poet Lord Byron, who had written:

> *Gods! how the glorious theme my strain exalts*
> *And rhyme finds partner rhyme in praise of 'Waltz' …*
> *Round all the confines of the yielded waist*
> *The strangest hand may wander undisplaced;*
> *The lady's in return may grasp as much*
> *As princely paunches may offer to her touch …*
> *Thus front to front the partners move or stand,*
> *The foot may rest, but none withdraw the hand …*
> *The breast thus publicly resign'd to man,*
> *In private may resist him – if it can.*

Strauss delayed announcing to his orchestra until towards the end of the stay in Paris that they were soon to leave for London. His logic was that he wanted nothing to upset the remaining concerts. On the other hand, as the final concert approached there was a palpable feeling of release among the men; soon they would be returning home to

Vienna. Predictably the simmering tension broke through to the surface when Strauss made his plans known. One particularly troublesome member of the orchestra, who led a small breakaway faction, convinced his supporters that if they once set foot on board a ship they would be parted from Europe for ever. He, and they, refused point-blank to follow Strauss.

Strauss took a two-pronged approach to the revolt. First he used attack as a means of defence, reminding the men they had all signed contracts, which he could hold them to. Secondly he stressed how he appreciated all the hard work they had done, how he admired their obvious devotion to him, and how he could guarantee them a pay increase based on the firm offers of work in England. Finally he said that after a lot of thought if any of them absolutely refused to travel further, he would release them from their contract and allow them to return home.

Four members of the orchestra left. It was thus a barely depleted party of musicians, Johann Strauss at their head, who boarded the appropriately named steamship *Princess Victoria* in the Dutch port of Flushing on the night of 11 April 1838 for the crossing to England, and the orchestra's biggest adventure yet.

Chapter 4

By Royal Appointment

I have used the word 'gruelling' to describe the schedule for Johann Strauss I and his orchestra in previous months. Now they were about to learn what that word really meant. Over the following nine months they would perform well over a hundred times, averaging around four concerts a week, constantly journeying throughout England north and south, as well as making trips to Scotland and Ireland. Strauss continued to compose, as well as directing the orchestra, responding to invitations, arranging travel, booking accommodation, and generally managing the lives – all the tensions, rivalries, minor disputes, unscheduled absences, occasional over-indulgence in alcohol, homesickness – of an orchestra on the road.

Small wonder the itinerary would end in total physical breakdown for Strauss, with London's leading musical journal, *The Musical World*, reporting (with a touch of malice): 'Strauss, who is on his hotel bed, finds himself successful, much applauded, very rich – and dying.'

It began badly. After a difficult overnight Channel crossing, Strauss found that the hotel he had booked in London's Leicester Square not only could not accommodate the entire party, causing some of the men to stay elsewhere, but it was also not clean, did not have a dining room, and the food was poor. To exacerbate matters Strauss discovered soon after checking in that a large sum of money, almost £100, had been stolen from his room.

There was nothing he could do immediately, since the first concert was scheduled in less than a week at the Queen's Concert Rooms in Hanover Square. His priority was arranging the programme and rehearsing. Strauss's mood was hardly improved when he learned that tickets were not selling well – poor weather, lack of advertising, a hit on at Covent Garden, and ridiculously expensive tickets at 10/6d.*

It is not hard to imagine the weariness with which Strauss must have mounted the podium, and the feeling of 'here we go again' among the players. That might account for the review in the following morning's *Times*, which accused Strauss of so drilling conformity and precision into his orchestra, that 'an effect is produced like that of an accurately constructed machine'.

---

* A comparison with today's prices is difficult, but a rough equivalent would be between £80 and £100.

Soon afterwards Strauss, known for his fieriness and quick temper, exploded. Things had got on top of him and the tour had barely started. He ordered his men to leave the awful hotel immediately, without giving due notice. The hotel proprietor, a certain George Street, took Strauss to court, and so Europe's most famous travelling composer and orchestral leader found himself up before a bewigged judge in London, in a scene that might well have inspired a young London author by the name of Charles Dickens.

Strauss was fortunate to escape with a fine of just £27 16s, but was ordered to pay court costs of £140, money that he did not have. Under Britain's notorious bankruptcy laws debtor prison beckoned for the whole entourage, which would have brought the nascent tour to an embarrassing and undignified end. The perilous situation was saved by a London music publisher named Robert Cocks, who offered to put the money up in return for the rights to publish Strauss's waltzes in Britain. Strauss knew this would cause problems with his Austrian publisher Tobias Haslinger, but reasoned that he had more chance of squaring things back in Vienna than in a strange city whose customs and laws were alien to him, whose people he did not know, and whose language he did not speak.

He therefore accepted Mr Cocks' offer, something for which the London publisher had reason to be grateful many times over in the coming years. The court case was resolved and the tour was back on.

Between that first concert on 17 April and the end of July, Strauss and his orchestra gave a total of seventy-nine performances in London alone, and the list of hosts for whom he performed reads like a *Who's Who* of English aristocracy: the Duke of Wellington, the Duke of Devonshire, the Duke of Cambridge, the Duke of Buccleuch and Sutherland, the Countess of Cadogan and Mrs Lionel de Rothschild, as well as the ambassadors of Austria and France. There were also two public balls, two charity concerts, thirty-nine public concerts, and three large-scale concerts shared with other high-profile artists.[*]

The ultimate accolade, though, came with the invitation to perform in the presence of the young Princess Victoria in Buckingham House, the building she was about to make her official royal palace. This took place on 10 May, and Strauss followed his usual practice of performing a piece specially composed for the occasion. This was the waltz '*Hommage à la Reine d'Angleterre*',[†] which tactfully quoted from '*Rule, Britannia*' in its introduction and '*God Save the Queen*' in waltz tempo in its coda. *The*

---

[*] At the ball given by the Duke of Sutherland, Strauss was also a guest, invited to join the Duke's table after the performance, a practice not uncommon in Paris or Vienna, but practically unheard of in the class-conscious milieu of Britain.

[†] Although the coronation of Queen Victoria was still six weeks away.

Times reported that Strauss's new waltz was much admired by the future queen, and thereafter Strauss made sure he included it in future performances following the coronation, both at the Palace and elsewhere on tour.

And what a tour he now embarked on. Even while resident in London, Strauss and the orchestra made a five-day visit to Cheltenham and Bath, and on leaving London at the end of July they began a six-week tour of England, Scotland and Ireland. In all they would perform in thirty-one different towns and cities, making return visits by popular demand to several of them.

On many days they gave three performances in three different venues: matinee, late afternoon, and evening. It was reported Strauss could now command fees of £200 or more for a performance – a substantial amount at that time. The constant travel was made easier by advances in modes of transport. Strauss himself wrote of the tour:

> *I found myself in a different town almost daily, as one may travel here exceedingly quickly by virtue of the good horses and excellent roads … Of great advantage to the traveller are the railways, which I have used extensively, in Liverpool, Manchester, Birmingham, etc. …*

But there was one feature of life in the United Kingdom over which Strauss could have no control: the weather. October in Scotland was cold and wet. There was a week of ceaseless rain, coaches had trouble making headway through the mud, and several members of the orchestra came down with colds or worse. A local doctor prescribed a concoction of claret, nutmeg and ginger, 'hot enough to wake the dead'. Still they performed. It was thus a group of musicians of depleted strength that made the crossing to Ireland, and all the more so on their return.

It was inevitable that sooner or later a work schedule of this intensity would catch up with Strauss and his men. It did so in the north of England. In November Strauss was reported to be suffering from 'illness of a serious character'. He had severe shivering fits, a hacking cough and chest pains. Concerts in Derby and Leicester were postponed. A doctor in Derby did little to improve things, by prescribing Strauss a dangerously strong dose of opium that almost killed him.

It is possible, even probable, that Strauss did not receive much sympathy from his men. This time they really had had enough. They had been away from home now for over a year, and they wanted to return to Vienna. A small but militant clique warned Strauss that if he did not promise that they would leave for home soon, they would refuse to play on.

There was another factor at work here, hidden not so far beneath the surface. The members of the orchestra were well aware of Johann Strauss's domestic arrangements back home in Vienna. He had a wife and children in the family home on the edge of the Augarten. He also had a mistress and illegitimate children in the apartment he had set up for them near St Stephen's Cathedral in the centre of the city.

Life for Strauss in Vienna was complicated. Life on tour, on the road, was an escape from all that. What if it was his plan, they conjectured, never to return? To stay away on tour for year after year. And how could he achieve that? Simple. By putting into action a plan he had mentioned more than once: the ultimate ambition. Board a ship for the United States. Succeed there, and there would be no need ever to return to Vienna and all the complications it held for him. Had he not implied as much when they were on tour in Ireland? Look west, he had told them, there is nothing between here and America. That is where we *must* go.

Strauss knew about the mutterings. He had a few faithful members of the orchestra who reported to him every nuance of what was being said. He also knew that, however much not returning to Vienna would solve domestic issues for him, he had no choice but to go back. He could not abrogate his responsibilities totally.

There was also the question of his health. He needed to consult with doctors who knew him and with whom he could at least converse in his own language. This latest bout of ill health had scared him. When the postponed concerts in Derby and Leicester had eventually taken place, he only had the strength to conduct the first half. That had not happened before. Something had to give.

It was therefore a relieved orchestra that was told by

Strauss that the tour was over and they would cross to Calais on the first leg of the return journey to Vienna. This they did on 2 December, almost eight months after arriving in England and fourteen months after leaving Vienna.

Strauss was not finished yet, though. It must have taken some persuasion on his part, and probably promises of increased remuneration, but he somehow managed to secure his orchestra's agreement to give a farewell concert in the rooms of the Philharmonic Society in Calais.

It did not go according to plan. In the third item on the programme he collapsed and fell from the podium. There was no swift recovery this time. He was taken to Paris where doctors warned him he needed substantial rest before making another move. He retorted that he was suffering from nothing more than exhaustion, and that after a few weeks of rest and recuperation he would be well enough to resume concerts – right there in Paris.

Reality dawned when he was informed that his orchestra was miles away, well advanced on their return to Vienna. This time, for the first time, he was no longer in control. Nor was his health improving. He lapsed into delirium several more times but was able to make it clear that he wished to return to Vienna to see his own doctors. There was agreement over this, not least because the last thing that the Paris doctors wanted was to preside over the demise of possibly the most famous musician in Europe.

A coach was fitted out with a bed and Strauss began the long journey home. The icy cold December air did nothing to improve his condition and, despite being piled high with blankets, he suffered a relapse in Strasbourg. Eventually the journey continued slowly, passing through Stuttgart, Ulm, Munich, and across the border into Austria. The one orchestral member who had stayed behind to accompany him reported an immediate improvement in his condition when he heard the Austrian accents in the town of Linz on the Danube. He arrived in Vienna three days before Christmas 1838, almost fifteen months since his departure. The *Theaterzeitung* reported, 'Strauss has at last arrived in Vienna, but suffering so much that it will be a considerable time before he is fully recovered.'

With typical bravado, even foolhardiness, Johann Strauss was back on the podium two weeks later, on 13 January 1839, at a ball in the Sperl, the dance hall he knew so well. For the occasion – again deploying the tactic at which he was so adept – he performed a piece he had composed specially for the occasion, '*Freuden-Grüsse (Motto: Überall gut – in der Heimath am besten)*', 'Joyful Greetings (Motto: Everywhere is good – at home is best)'.

Johann Strauss was welcomed back rapturously by his many admirers, his most loyal fans. To them he was a returning hero. Word had regularly come back to Vienna of how the English, considered snobbish, inimical to foreign influences, had taken him to their hearts. And had their own Johann not performed for the young Queen Victoria? Who could match that, not just from Vienna, but from any other country in Europe? Strauss, the most famous musician in Europe, and he was theirs.

Strauss must have wished it were that simple. He had, of course, come home to his messy and complicated domestic arrangements. Meanwhile much had changed during the fifteen months of his absence. The Vienna he returned to was a different city to the one he had left all those months ago. The change was not overt, but it was there.

The chancellor, Klemens von Metternich, had tightened his grip on the city. He needed to. His network of spies had never been so busy. There was a dangerous mood, an undercurrent, that was gaining strength. Students, writers, poets and playwrights were writing material they knew to be seditious, dangerous, liable to lead to their arrest.

As a new decade dawned, so did a new feeling that the repression of the last twenty or more years could not endure. Whispers became voices. The cosy domesticity of the Biedermeier era contained within itself the inevitable seeds of change. We know now, with the benefit of hindsight, that it would be just a few more years before change would come, and that when it did it would explode with a force that would change Europe for ever.

What Johann Strauss could not in his most fantastical dreams have imagined was that when change did come, it would not only sweep away the established order, it would take him along with it.

Chapter 5

A Family Conspiracy

It was not just a different Vienna that Johann Strauss returned to, but a subtly altered set – or sets – of domestic circumstances. It appears Strauss did not just prefer the company of his mistress and illegitimate family, but had developed an intense disregard for his wife and legitimate children.

While he was abroad on tour he had used an intermediary to send large amounts of money – secretly – to Emilie Trampusch. On his return he moved back into the large family house, the Hirschenhaus, but lived in a separate apartment within it. Whether he insisted on this arrangement, or Anna banished him to his own quarters, is not known. Quite probably it was Johann's doing, since the apartment gave him room to live and work: he could compose there, he had an office from which to run the orchestra's complicated schedule, and in the large main room there was space actually to rehearse with his players. Anna would also have been forced to rely on him for housekeeping money. He held the purse strings, literally.

His wife's public humiliation was made complete by the fact that in the seven years after his return to Vienna he fathered a further five children with Emilie. He might have lived in the family house but he clearly spent a lot of time in the Kumpfgasse. The atmosphere in the Hirschenhaus, at least when Strauss was there, must have been tense, to say the least. He was not happy in the company of his family, and the clear dislike he had for his wife was something he also exhibited towards his children.

The two elder boys were developing a talent for playing the piano, and Johann II would recall in later years how he and Josef would watch their father conduct orchestral rehearsals in the house, 'paying close attention to every note, so that we familiarised ourselves with his style and then played what we heard straight off, in exactly the same spirited manner as he had. He was our ideal.'

The admiration was not reciprocated. Johann said his father had no idea his two sons were talented pianists and that when they finally demonstrated their skills to him, he accused them of 'tinkling at the keys in an amateurish fashion'.

Their father went further. There was to be no thought on either of their parts of a career in music. He would not allow it. Instead they were to continue with normal school studies. And so in 1841, when Johann was fifteen and Josef thirteen, they were enrolled as students in the Commercial

Studies Department of the Polytechnic Institute of Vienna. Strauss planned a career in banking for his eldest son, and engineering for the younger.

Johann II, at least, had other plans, and he confided in his closest ally, his mother. He was in no doubt that he wanted his future to be in music. Furthermore he had no intention of becoming a banker, nor did he intend remaining at the Polytechnic Institute. His mother, it appears, sided entirely with him, and it is not difficult to understand why. In the first place Johann's musical talent was blindingly obvious, and his father's refusal to see it must have been deliberate obstinacy. The boy had actually composed his first waltz at the age of six and given the manuscript page with a mere twenty-one bars of a simple melody in three-four time to an impressed mother.

Now, at the same time as attending the Polytechnic Institute and with money in the household in short supply, he was giving music lessons to children of friends. He was himself just fifteen years of age, and he was already bringing in funds with his natural talent at the piano.

Probably too there was the feeling at the back of Anna's mind that to do something surreptitious, that her husband was unaware of, would be somehow getting back at him for the hurt he had caused her. And what if her eldest son proved to have real musical talent? Wouldn't that be a delicious irony? What better way for her and her family to avenge themselves than by outstripping her husband in the very area in which he excelled?

So when Johann came to his mother and said he wanted to give up his studies and devote himself to music, he found a willing and accommodating pair of ears. There was more to Johann's plan. He did not want simply to become a musician so that he could perform at the piano, or earn a living giving piano lessons. Oh no, his mind was set on greater things. He had observed his father and learned from him. He admired what his father was doing in music. He might not have enjoyed anything approaching a close father–son relationship, but his father – unwittingly – was providing him with knowledge and inspiration, and his son, even at the tender age of fifteen, knew exactly what use he intended to make of this.

He turned to his mother. He wanted to learn the violin. He knew his father would never agree to this. He wanted to reach a level of proficiency where he could form his own orchestra and give concerts of his own compositions. In other words, to follow exactly in his father's musical footsteps. He assured his mother that he could pay for lessons with the money his own teaching was bringing in. Anna willingly entered the conspiracy and went straight into the enemy camp, as it were, by approaching one Franz Amon, first violinist in her husband's own orchestra, who deputised for him on occasion as conductor with a second group when Strauss himself was on tour.

Clearly Anna knew Amon well enough to know that he would not divulge the plan to her husband. She was right. Amon agreed to teach the young Johann, and to keep it secret from his employer. Discretion was obviously paramount but an indication of just how little interest Strauss took in his children is evidenced by the fact that Johann left the Polytechnic Institute within a year to take lessons from Amon and devote himself full time to music, and his father had no idea.

It was a fairly remarkable act of faith on the part of Franz Amon. He was presumably risking his job in teaching a teenager who seemed to have a precocious musical talent, but can hardly have yet shown signs of the compositional genius he would later display. It is possible Amon had some grudge against Strauss senior, or even that he disapproved of Strauss's treatment of his family.

Whatever lay behind it, Amon not only began giving Johann secret lessons, he also tutored him in exactly the skills of his father – not simply to play the violin, but to stand up and sway in time to the music, in effect to lead from the violin. He also taught him to perform the three-four rhythm of the waltz, to create a yearning and languid phrase, to slow down towards the middle, to give just a moment's hiatus at the high point of the melody before continuing – all details that would later instantly identify a piece as being by Johann Strauss the Younger.

Amon was, of course, able to do this only because of Johann's innate and extraordinary musical talent, which the older man quickly recognised. He soon realised, too, that there would come a point when he no longer had anything to teach Johann, particularly in the field of composition, and so after a while he passed Johann on first to an organist who was an experienced composer, and then to a professional violin teacher who played at the Vienna Court Opera.

Johann Strauss II was becoming a seriously good violinist, with a natural talent for composition, and in a city such as Vienna this could not stay secret for long. Sooner or later word was bound to reach his father, and reach him it did. Johann recalled later in life that one fine day he was playing the violin in front of a mirror in his room, swaying as he played, ascertaining which particular bodily movements were more elegant than others, when the door opened and his father walked in.

'What?' Johann recalled his father shouting. 'You play the violin?' Johann said his father had heard on the musical grapevine that he had ambitions to become a professional musician, but regarded it as a ridiculous idea since he had no idea in the first place that his son even played the violin. According to the son there was 'a violent and unpleasant scene'. He apparently tried to reason with his father, to interest him in his aims, but his father 'wanted to know nothing of my plans'.

One can imagine the hurt this must have caused the teenage boy. Every boy hoping to follow in his father's footsteps wants to make him proud, and the total rejection must have seriously wounded him. It is true that Johann was recalling the incident many years after it happened, but the actions that Strauss would go on to take suggest that Johann was not exaggerating. In fact it is hard to believe that a father could be as callous, uncaring and vindictive as Strauss was about to show himself to be.

Strauss senior spared barely a thought for his precociously talented eldest son. He had no need to. He had never been as busy or as popular. In the first half of the new decade he made guest appearances with his orchestra in Austria, Hungary, Austrian Silesia, Saxony, Prussia and Germany, as well as fulfilling numerous engagements in Vienna.

In 1843 his former friend and rival Joseph Lanner, the only other musician who had ever come anywhere close to challenging him, died of typhus infection two days after his forty-second birthday. Johann Strauss now stood alone as composer and orchestra leader, the undisputed master of his genre in the city of music. To cement this unrivalled reputation, he was about to earn the title 'Waltz King' with the most masterly waltz he had composed to date, the '*Lorelei-Rhein-Klänge*' ('Echoes of the Rhine Lorelei'). The opening phrase, crowned with a *fortissimo* chord, then repeated, immediately secured the audience's attention, before the waltz launched into a melody so beguiling it was soon being whistled and hummed on the streets of Vienna.

Vienna had its Waltz King. It was Johann Strauss the Elder. Nothing and no one could displace him.

No one except his namesake: his eldest son. Johann II was about to launch a challenge, one that could, potentially, hardly be more devastating or humiliating. But a challenge was all it was. Strauss had nothing to fear. His son had a modicum of talent, nothing more. He most certainly did not have either the talent or the resources to see his challenge become reality.

And what was this challenge? Strauss could hardly believe it when he heard about it. On 3 August 1844, a year and two months short of his twentieth birthday, Johann Strauss the Younger, armed with excellent testimonials from his two highly respected teachers, approached the Viennese authorities with an extraordinary request:

> *I intend to play with an orchestra of twelve to fifteen players in restaurants, specifically at Dommayer's in Hietzing, whose manager has already assured me that I can hold musical entertainments there as soon as my orchestra is in order. I have not yet determined the remaining venues, but I believe I will be able to secure sufficient engagements and income …*

Johann was being nothing if not bold. As yet he had no orchestra worthy of the name. He did the rounds of taverns where itinerant musicians played, particularly the Zur Stadt Belgrad ('At the City of Belgrade'), which was well known for its musical entertainment. He hired musicians, trained them, dismissed some, kept others, engaged more.

On 5 September Johann junior was probably as surprised as anyone when the municipal council granted his request. He now showed himself to be his father's son. A month later, calling himself 'Herr Kapellmeister Johann Strauss',* he drew up a carefully worded one-year contract with twenty-four musicians, detailing the rights and obligations of the parties under eight separate sections, including rules on punctuality and discipline at rehearsals and performances, as well as details of how issues such as illness, prohibition of substitutes, settlement of disputes, even the careful handling of musical instruments, should be dealt with.

From the very moment he put together an orchestra, Johann Strauss the Younger left no one in any doubt as to who was in charge. It was his orchestra, not just in substance, but in name too, and woe betide any musician who thought otherwise.

There were now two Johann Strauss orchestras in Vienna. One was thoroughly professional, with many tours behind it, garlanded wherever it went. The other was a motley bunch of ill-trained musicians with little or no experience, who had never played together before, certainly not in an orchestra of this size, with no understanding of the discipline and cooperation it would require.

Furthermore, while Strauss senior could command the most prestigious dance halls in Vienna, it appeared his son had secured a tavern in the suburb of Hietzing, opposite

---

* Not easily translatable. The closest might be 'Concert Master and Conductor', or 'Music Director'. At any rate, the most senior musician.

the Schönbrunn park, with the unsophisticated name of Dommayer's Casino. It was practically out of town. No one who really mattered would bother to make the journey. The audience would be regulars enjoying a drink and a chat.

Johann Strauss senior was confident he had nothing to fear from his precocious and overly ambitious son. Just as well, because his attention was diverted in another direction. Anna Strauss, fed up with her husband's misbehaviour and emboldened by her son's extraordinary courage and willpower, sued for divorce.

Chapter 6

'Good Morning, Strauss Son*!'*

There was a lot of ill will, venom even, flying around over Johann the Younger's proposed debut concert, and it was entirely in one direction – from father to son. Legends have abounded from that day to this of the measures Strauss took to prevent his son's concert from even taking place.

It was said he sent a loyal colleague around all the main dance halls to tell the manager that if Johann was allowed to stage his concert there, he – the famous Strauss – would never perform there again. It is more than likely something of the sort took place since, although Dommayer's was hardly a prime venue, Strauss, who had played there many times in the past, was never to do so again.

Tickets for the concert were selling extremely well, despite the relative difficulty of getting to the venue. Strauss senior, stunned by this news, came to the conclusion his son was achieving this by sheer fraud. The posters advertising the concert had the name JOHANN STRAUSS in large capital letters in bold print, with the word *Sohn* ['Son'] in small letters, not bold, in brackets underneath. Strauss and his supporters accused Johann of deliberately trying to pass himself off as his father, to ensure a good audience.

Unable to prevent the concert from taking place despite his claims, Strauss senior announced that he would give a concert on the same evening. In the end this did not materialise, possibly because ticket sales had gone so well that he feared his own concert might be less well attended than his son's.

The most persistent legend is that Strauss, with the help of that same loyal colleague, organised a 'claque', a group of supporters to attend the younger Johann's concert and disrupt it. This seems an unnaturally harsh course of action for a father to take against his son. But should there be any doubt about the sheer antagonism Strauss felt towards Johann, he summed it up himself in a comment he made to his publisher on the Sunday before the concert: 'I hope I don't live to see Tuesday.'

Despite the worst Strauss could do, interest in Johann's concert was not just intense; it had reached something approaching fever pitch. The journal *Der Wanderer* reported that getting a seat for Johann's debut was as difficult as getting a seat in the House of Lords in the British Parliament.

Why might this be? Well, Johann was due to turn nineteen years of age ten days after his debut concert. He had been taking violin lessons for around four years, first from

Strauss's own first violinist and later from a senior violinist at the Vienna Court Opera. He had also been receiving instruction in harmony and counterpoint from a music professor who ran his own private music school, and then with a certain Joseph Drechsler, organist and choirmaster at the Am Hof church, shortly to be appointed kapellmeister at St Stephen's Cathedral, composer of around thirty-five operas and musical comedies, and one of the most respected musicians in Vienna.

In other words, Johann's musical talent was not exactly unknown in Vienna's musical circles. More than that, word was spreading fast, accompanied no doubt by a raft of superlatives. The fact that he shared the name and bloodline of Vienna's most famous orchestral leader was causing excitement among the city's *cognoscenti* long before the announcement of his inaugural concert.

Those facts alone would surely have been sufficient to guarantee a respectably sized audience at Dommayer's. But underlying this commendable musical inquisitiveness was an understandable, if slightly dubious, desire to pay Strauss back for his appalling behaviour towards his legitimate family. Everyone with even the smallest interest in musical matters was aware of his attempts to stop his eldest son pursuing his talent for music, of how Johann had formed an orchestra despite his father's opposition, and secured permission from the authorities to hold the concert. They will have known, too, of the efforts Strauss had gone to in the hope of ensuring the concert failed.

Knowledge of his unconventional domestic life was widespread – of his many illegitimate children, his wife's humiliation. A woman suing for divorce was almost unheard of at that time, but Anna did not need to fear that her decision would rebound against her. There was universal sympathy for her situation and the divorce was granted with no complications.

Whatever the motive – and for many it might have been no more than the chance to enjoy an evening of music in the gardens around Dommayer's on a lovely autumn evening – there was a steady stream of concertgoers leaving the centre of the city, passing through the gates of the massive city wall, the Bastei, across the green spaces of the Glacis, and out towards the suburb of Hietzing. Some reports said people left the city in their thousands, though hundreds seems more likely.

Such was the crush inside Dommayer's that attempts by waiters to serve food and drink were quickly abandoned, a fact resented by several music critics, threatening to darken their mood before a note had been played.

Johann himself confessed later to feeling sick with fright as he waited to go out onto the stage. He was convinced of failure, fearful even that he might be laughed off stage. He had no idea how many of his father's supporters were in the audience, or how vocal they might be.

He knew he already had one fact militating against success. His orchestra consisted of a mere fifteen musicians, nothing like the size of his father's orchestra. He had rehearsed them as well as he could, but how much could be done in a matter of weeks? With personnel changes and other administrative problems, serious rehearsal had probably not taken place for more than a matter of days.

But he knew the biggest hurdle lay with his own compositions. He had put together a programme of music by established composers – Meyerbeer, Auber, von Suppé – as well as pieces of his own.* It was these pieces he would be judged by. Orchestral players come and go. If the orchestra was not up to scratch, he would sooner or later be able to improve it. Critics were aware of that. What the critics wanted to know, above all, was how good a composer Johann himself was, even at this early age. A good showing, and they could presume he would follow in his father's footsteps. If his compositions were not up to the mark, well, there was time for improvement, but he would probably be unlikely to progress beyond being a band leader. Good composers started young.

There might well have been a small gasp of recognition as Johann walked self-consciously out onto the stage. The same hair, jet black and curly, as his famous father, dark gleaming eyes, and a similar swagger of self-confidence, even if it masked an inner nervousness. The clothes, too, no less flamboyant than his father's – blue tailcoat with silver buttons, embroidered silk waistcoat, grey trousers

---

* An exact list of the pieces played is not known, though the compositions I mention by Johann Strauss most certainly were. No newspaper carried the full programme, and no programmes have survived.

looped under buckled shoes – even if they were, as rumour had it, borrowed for the night.

The similarity went much further, as one reviewer remarked in print the following day. Not just a similar facial expression, but the way he held and played his violin, the bow grasped with the tips of the fingers, graceful gestures of the lower part of the arm, swift energetic bowing. And, in the most noticeable influence of his father, a sudden turning to the audience, spraying sparks from his violin 'as if from a galvanic battery'. This was the son, proving as adept and mesmerising a performer as his father. So far.

A polite, respectful reception for works by other composers. But Johann braced himself for what he knew was the most important moment of his nascent musical career. He had scheduled a waltz of his own. Originally entitled '*Das Mutterherz*' ('The Heart of a Mother') in tribute to the one person who had made it possible for him to pursue his dream, the sensible and down-to-earth Anna had persuaded him to alter it. He chose '*Die Gunstwerber*' ('Seekers of Favour').

Johann raised the violin and settled it comfortably under his chin. The whole top part of his body bent into the opening triplet of chords, played *fortissimo*. The audience could not but pay attention. The chords repeated, leading into a gentle lyrical passage which itself led into as beguiling a waltz as this audience had heard, instantly as charming as anything his father had written. Turning at the *crescendo* to face the audience, forcing them to sway with him, he looked back to the orchestra, before turning again and playing a beautiful, melodious solo passage on the violin, gazing out at the audience and smiling as he did so.

They were mesmerised. Another waltz theme, before returning to the first that had followed the opening chords, this time met with a smile of recognition by the audience. Solo violin again, played as if for each individual member of the audience, leading to a final quickened flourish calculated to bring on applause.

Which it most certainly did. Applause and more applause. An encore, and another, and another. Johann had to repeat '*Die Gunstwerber*' no fewer than four times. After that he could do no wrong. More pieces by established composers, then another waltz of his own, '*Die Sinngedichte*' ('Poems of the Senses'). Contemporary reports said this piece had to be repeated *nineteen* times. Whether an exaggeration or not, the message was clear. Johann junior had triumphed.

But the single most moving moment of the whole evening came quite unexpectedly, catching the audience unaware. It was a calculated gesture on Johann's part, which he had rehearsed with his orchestra. It needed no introduction. There must have been a collective gasp of recognition as the orchestra played the opening bars of Strauss senior's latest and most popular work, '*Lorelei-Rhein-Klänge*'.

The import was not lost on the audience. This was son paying tribute to father, a younger man acknowledging the musical debt he owed to his father. Johann had not simply triumphed, he had done so without rancour, and he had done so on his own terms. The piece had to be repeated three times.

For those who could not be at Dommayer's that evening, the music critics of Vienna left them in no doubt as to what they had missed, and they were unanimous in their praise.

Ernst Decsey, music historian and music critic of the *Neues Wiener Tagblatt*, said of Johann's '*Die Gunstwerber*' that it was 'as if singing had broken out from all three storeys of the house', and that it contained 'the same modest *piano*, the same reverberating *forte*, as the father … Basses rumble, intermediate parts woo, and the main violin theme vibrates across to the ladies.' Strauss senior had never received a more laudatory accolade for one of his compositions.

Another critic, Johann Nepomuk Vogt, made a direct comparison between father and son. Complaining in the *Österreichisches Morgenblatt* of being pushed and jostled by the crowd, of nearly suffocating and being deprived of food and drink, he found the energy to write:

> *Talent is the monopoly of no single individual. This young man is fully as melodious, as piquant, as effective in his instrumentation as his father … and yet he is no slavish imitator of the elder Strauss's methods of composition.*

The *Wiener Allgemeine Theaterzeitung*, after praising the irresistible and popular style of Johann's own compositions, reported that in playing '*Lorelei-Rhein-Klänge*', Johann 'gave expression not only to a son's admiration for his father, but also to his desire to take his father's long-standing mastery as his example'.

Perhaps the most perceptive of the reviews came from Franz Wiest, music critic of *Der Wanderer*. After commenting that it is seldom that the gifts and talents of a father are passed on to a son, he stated:

> *Of Strauss son one really can say:* He is a waltz incarnate! ... *The two waltz pieces he performed for us today distinguished themselves by their brilliant originality of thought, vibrating with that rhythmical flourish and glowing with that Viennese lightheartedness which, with the exception of Strauss father, no living waltz composer can create.*

In a direct comparison between the two Strausses, from which the father emerges the loser, Wiest wrote, 'Strauss son, at the age of twenty-one [*sic*], has learned more as a composer and conductor than Strauss father could have gained in twenty-one years in his field ...' However, he stressed this should not be seen as a reproach. Instead Vienna should rejoice in the fact it now had a Strauss father and a Strauss son in its midst.

Remembering this was the year following the death of Joseph Lanner, Wiest ended his review with a short sentence that has entered musical history, as far-sighted in its way as Beethoven's teacher comparing him at the age of just sixteen to Mozart: 'Good Night *Lanner*! Good Evening *Strauss Father*! Good Morning *Strauss Son*!'

Wiest's words were prophetic. There were indeed two Strausses now in Vienna. It was a fact that Strauss senior had no choice but to accept. Did it in any way mollify his attitude to his son? If anything, it hardened it. The rivalry he had perhaps feared only subconsciously was now there for anyone with a modicum of musical intelligence to see – which meant, embarrassingly for him, practically the whole of Vienna.

Life did not change overnight for either father or son. But before the decade was out Vienna would be a new city, very different from the one that had seen that concert at Dommayer's.

The undercurrents of fear and suspicion that had been slowly fomenting in Europe since the end of the Napoleonic wars were soon to give way to outright revolution. There was discontent from the bottom up. The working classes resented the wealth and influence of the aristocracy; the aristocracy in turn resented the absolute power of monarchy.

Technological advances were transforming workers' lives, and in several European countries an increasingly liberal press was campaigning for better conditions and higher wages.

Open discontent first seeped out onto the streets in Paris and other French cities, and workers and students in other countries were quick to follow suit. Vienna, in particular, was about to catch fire and Metternich would feel the full force of popular fury.

Given the power and speed with which revolutionary fervour swept Europe, it is perhaps surprising that it produced few lasting effects. The uprisings were ultimately nothing more sophisticated than an attempt at mob rule; long on enthusiasm and very short indeed on organisation.

Vienna though was something of an exception. True, the revolution was brutally put down, but not before Metternich and his wife fled the city under cover of darkness. Before the year was out there would be a new emperor on the Habsburg throne, a much younger man than before and one who was more likely to respond to the discontent.

This was a monumental change at the time, albeit less perceptible a few years on. What was entirely new, though, was an attitude, an empowerment. The working classes, who had never been heard before, now had a voice, even if it was somewhat muted.

It was the beginning of a new era – in music as well as in so much else. Vienna had a new emperor, and a new Waltz King.

Chapter 7

Radetzky Marches Out of Step

It began with a relatively insignificant incident. It was an act of violence, resulting in unnecessary deaths, but it could have been contained. As had happened before and would happen again, this was the spark that lit a tinderbox of anger and discontent.

At one o'clock on Monday, 13 March 1848, a small detachment of soldiers fired a volley of shots into a motley crowd of students, workers and general malcontents who had forced their way past heavy gates into the courtyard outside the Lower Austrian Landhaus. Their orders had been to fire warning shots above the heads of the demonstrators, but they panicked and fired directly into the crowd.

At least five fell dead and many more were wounded. What could have remained a little local trouble rapidly escalated. Angry demonstrators broke into the city armoury.

Outside the city gates, which had been closed, government buildings were smashed, machinery destroyed, and factories set on fire.

By the end of the day several dozen people had been killed. It was enough to precipitate a series of events that would change Vienna and Austria for ever. The demands of the demonstrators were the culmination of more than thirty years of repression. In themselves they were not particularly extreme: freedom of the press, public accounting of government expenditure, an end to constantly rising food prices, more representation for the middle classes in government.

But they were, in effect, a declaration of war against the rule of law, and the chancellor who had single-handedly and ruthlessly imposed it for the past several decades: Klemens von Metternich.

Beyond their domestic demands, there was something else on the malcontents' agenda: an end to Austrian rule in northern Italy. Unlikely though it might seem, this demand would have a direct impact on the lives of the city's most famous musical dynasty, dividing the Strauss family down the middle, older generation against younger, in a way from which it would never recover.

As part of the Austrian empire's expansionist policy, its army was in occupation of northern Italy. With Vienna in disarray the order soon went south to the commander of the Austrian army not to engage the Italian nationalist forces but to maintain a ceasefire. The commander ignored the order and engaged the Italians at Custozza, where he scored a decisive victory on 24 and 25 July.

Milan and Lombardy were preserved for the empire, to the joy of the old guard in Vienna. But while the governing class and the military celebrated, the revolutionaries vented their disgust. What right did Austria have to occupy any territory beyond its borders? Their anger increased when the Austrian army went on to further victories, shoring up Austrian rule across northern Italy.

Such was the joy, though, in the mansions and stately homes of the Establishment that the decision was made to honour the Austrian commander and his army with a 'Grand Impressive Victory Festival' to be held on the Wasserglacis, the wide expanse of green outside the city wall.

Johann Strauss senior was commissioned to compose a new piece in honour of the Austrian commander, which he gladly accepted. What better way to establish his pre-eminent position above all fellow composers in Vienna, including his own son?

The celebrations were planned for 31 August, and so time was short. Strauss took two Viennese folk songs, re-worked them, and composed a new piece in the form of a march. Legend has it that it took him just two hours to compose the piece, which given how prodigious he was might well be true, or at least not too much of an exaggeration.

Strauss named the piece, naturally, for the man in whose honour he had written it. That was the eighty-two-year-old commander-in-chief of the Austrian army, Field-Marshal Johann Josef Wenzel, Count Radetzky von Radetz.

Strauss could not have known it at the time, but that swiftly written little piece would ensure his immortality. The instantly catchy tune, the bouncing rhythm; it is practically impossible not to tap one's fingers, or stamp one's feet, in time to the music. In fact it is traditional – not just in Vienna, but across the globe – to clap in time to the music. It is, of course, the world-famous *'Radetzky March'*.

The two Johann Strausses, father and son, were divided emotionally and professionally. The son resented the father for walking out and shamelessly starting a second family. Now each was running his own orchestra, competing for dates in the same venues. To make matters worse, when workers and students took to the streets of Vienna in the revolution of 1848, father and son took opposing sides. Strauss senior, now in middle age, instinctively supported the old regime, the established order. His *'Radetzky March'* commission cemented this.

Johann, his son, saw things very differently, on several occasions actually leading his band to the barricades. Like most young men of his age he wanted change, and change was what was happening. Within days of the fatal shootings on 13 March, the unthinkable happened.

Chancellor Metternich, who had until this point been able to rely on the total support of the Habsburg monarchy, now found that support haemorrhaging away. The ineffectual emperor, beset with ill health, allowed others around him to wield power, and they needed a scapegoat. They found it in the man who had governed so ruthlessly for decades but now found that events were slipping from his control. The chancellor must resign, they declared. And not just resign, but flee the city and the country. The Metternich era was over.*

Johann made no secret of his sympathies for the revolutionaries, among whom he had many friends. In May he became kapellmeister of the National Guard, which sided with the students, and composed a string of numbers with titles such as *'Revolutions-Marsch'* ('Revolution March'), *'Barrikaden-Lieder'* ('Songs of the Barricades'), which he retitled *'Freiheits-Lieder'* ('Songs of Freedom'), and *'Burschen-Lieder'* ('Students' Songs').

Both Johann and Josef spent at least some time helping man the barricades, and Johann found himself briefly under arrest in December for playing *'La Marseillaise'* in public, a clear sign of support for fellow revolutionaries in Paris. In his defence he stated that there was no political or nationalistic motive behind any piece he chose to play; in fact he had done his best to

---

* An exact list of the pieces played is not known, though the compositions I mention by Johann Strauss most certainly were. No newspaper carried the full programme, and no programmes have survived.

avoid controversy. Somewhat disingenuously he blamed the demands of the audience, who he feared might riot if he did not satisfy their demands. The case against him was dropped.

On 2 December 1848, in case anyone doubted that change was truly happening, the feeble emperor abdicated, and his nephew Franz Josef became Emperor of Austria. The old guard resented the change, pointing to the fact that Franz Josef was a mere eighteen years of age, trained for the military not government, and would be deposed, or forced to abdicate, within a short while.

In fact Franz Josef – 'Franzl' – would reign for almost sixty-eight years, almost the longest-ruling monarch in European history. He would live into the First World War, and preside over the downfall of the House of Habsburg. In his lifetime he would have to endure more personal tragedy than any man or woman should ever have to know.

His long life would also, at several points, intersect with that of the musician whose compositions would define his reign, the man who, in a single piece of music around ten minutes long, would provide a greater insight into the character of Franz Josef than many hundreds of pages of biography.

But that still lay in the future. Now, as the mid-point in the turbulent nineteenth century approached, a truly new era in Vienna was dawning. The Viennese knew it; so did their new emperor. Young Johann Strauss and his brothers were in no doubt. The same could not entirely be said of their father.

Johann Strauss senior took his orchestra back on tour, and an extensive tour it was. He needed to get out of Vienna. In the wake of the demonstrations and violence the people were restless. The annual new-year carnival, the *Fasching*, was a lacklustre affair in 1849. The populace wanted more than concerts to appease them. And, whether he liked it or not, Strauss was associated with the old regime, the past that had gone for ever. Was he not, after all, the composer of the *'Radetzky March'*?

He took his orchestra first to Prague, and was stunned when protesters gathered outside his hotel chanting revolutionary slogans. He had never been the target of political demonstrations before. He was, simply, a musician.

At the performance the night following his arrival, he made a decision that went against every artistic fibre in his body. He was acting on advice, though he could scarcely believe he was following it. For the sake of public order, he dropped the *'Radetzky March'* from the programme. And still there were boos interlaced with the cheers.

After a brief return to Vienna, he left with the orchestra – thirty-two strong – for Germany. There, at least, he could be sure of a warm welcome, if past experience was anything to go by. But nothing was the same: the glory days were over.

Ulm and Munich in Bavaria, traditional, Catholic areas, close to Austria, were warm towards him, but as he travelled west and north, the hostility grew. Augsburg, Stuttgart, Heidelberg, Heilbronn, Mannheim, Mainz, Koblenz, Bonn, Cologne, Aachen. To some degree or other, it seemed, no matter where he went, he encountered hostility.

Even though he had dropped the '*Radetzky March*' from the programme, even distributing cockades in the republican colours of black, red and gold for his men to pin to their Old German hats. But it made no difference. He was a black-and-yellow, whether he liked it or not – the colours of the Habsburg monarchy. The old days of adoring crowds were gone.

Nowhere was it worse than in Frankfurt. The audience shouted 'Berlioz! Berlioz!' and demanded the '*Rakoczy March*', a traditional Hungarian march that Berlioz had popularised by including it in his *La damnation de Faust*. The irony of the similarity in names of the two pieces cannot have been lost on Strauss. In the event he played neither. Nor can he have failed to remember the rapturous reception the same Berlioz had given to his music in Paris ten years earlier.

A deep depression settled over Johann Strauss I. His music was being rejected. *He* was being rejected. There were domestic problems at home in Vienna, political issues on tour, and his finances were anything but secure. He wrote to music publishers, booksellers and music agents in advance of his arrival to ask them to arrange accommodation, concert venues and publicity. He told them in letters that he could not afford to stay in any particular town without a guaranteed number of performances.

He was pleased to get out of Germany and head down the Rhine into Belgium, where the reception in Brussels, Antwerp and Ostend was more along the lines he was used to. The farther he travelled from home, the less his association with the old regime mattered.

There was one destination where he could be sure of a truly warm welcome, where his political affiliations, if anything, would count in his favour. Eleven years earlier he and his orchestra had been lauded and lionised, and he knew he could count on the same again. On the night of 21 April 1849, he and his orchestra crossed the Channel to England.

He need not have worried about securing enough engagements. London, Reading, Oxford, Cheltenham, with many repeat visits. In a stay of two and a half months the Strauss Orchestra gave a total of forty-six performances, not far short of five concerts a week for ten weeks. A truly gruelling schedule.

The highlight, as before, was a performance at Buckingham Palace in the presence of Queen Victoria and Prince Albert. This was at a state ball before 1,600 guests, and for the occasion Strauss had composed his *'Alice-Polka'* in honour of the queen's six-year-old daughter.

Other new compositions were performed at other venues, and at Exeter Hall in London Strauss shared the stage with a Viennese singer making her first visit to England.

She was described in a London newspaper as 'a handsome woman, with a ripe mezzo-soprano voice, a charming style, and great dramatic feeling'.

The singer was Jetty Treffz, though that was not her real name, and she will re-enter our story in a most dramatic and unexpected way in thirteen years' time.

The reception Strauss received was a throwback to the old days: applause, cheers, encores. He was moving in the very highest circles of the English aristocracy, who took their lead from the queen herself. Such was his popularity with the upper classes that several members of the royal family and the nobility took it on themselves to organise a 'Farewell Matinée Musicale' at the end of the tour for Strauss's benefit 'as proof of their satisfaction of the admirable manner in which he has conducted the music at their balls and soirées this season'.

The Duchesses of Gloucester, Cambridge and Mecklenburg-Strelitz personally undertook the sale of tickets. Strauss also paid a visit on the exiled Prince Metternich and his wife, no doubt reminiscing about the old days, and how things would never be the same again in Vienna.

Political events back home in Vienna seemed not to trouble Strauss's English hosts. The *Morning Post* reported with English *hauteur*:

> *If the revolutionary mania of Austria has unsettled Germany, at least England has no reason to lament the political mischief …*

And it found itself beguiled by the Viennese Waltz King:

> *Time has dealt kindly with him, for his broad, honest Teutonic face is still full of intelligence, and his fire and energy have not a jot abated.*

To some extent, though, the newspaper had allowed the dazzling exterior that Strauss wore like comfortable clothing to obscure the truth that lay beneath. Strauss remained depressed. Pained and tortured by the hostility shown towards him closer to home, he wrote anguished letters to close friends in Vienna. To Emilie he prophesied that this would be his last tour.

Once again, the strain of a relentless schedule, coupled with the chill and damp of the English climate, had affected his health. A flotilla of small boats that accompanied him and his orchestra as it sailed out of the Thames Estuary might have lifted his spirits temporarily, but it was an exhausted, depressed, unwell Johann Strauss who arrived back on 14 July at the small apartment in Vienna where, now a divorced man, he lived openly with Emilie and their five children.

Within days of his return,* Strauss was back on the podium

---

* Some reports give the date as 15 July, the night after his return, though this seems unlikely.

in front of his orchestra at Unger's Casino. Legend has it that in the first piece, the overture to the new opera *Maritana* by William Vincent Wallace, Strauss's bow snapped. The audience gasped at this ill omen. It is likely that the legend is an exaggeration. Maybe a string on his violin snapped. Maybe the ill omen came into being in the knowledge of what was to follow.

There are no reports, as far as I can tell, of how the performance went, what other pieces were played, whether Strauss was visibly unwell. What is certain, though, is that this was Johann Strauss's last concert.

In the late summer of 1849 the victorious Field-Marshal Radetzky returned from Italy to a hero's welcome from the old guard, who were once more in control after the failure of the street revolutions of the year before. A grand banquet in his honour was planned for 22 September in the Redoutensaal, the huge ceremonial hall of the Hofburg Palace, seat of the emperor.

Johann Strauss was engaged for the event. He and his orchestra were to provide suitable musical entertainment for the distinguished guests. Strauss would, naturally, perform his famous *'Radetzky March'*, as well as a newly commissioned work in the Field-Marshal's honour, the *'Radetzky-Bankett-Marsch'* ('Radetzky Banquet March').

But it was not to be. Strauss's health had worsened, and a telltale rash spreading across his body was diagnosed as scarlet fever. For the rest of her life Strauss's illegitimate daughter Clementina, eleven years old in the summer of

1849, blamed herself for passing on the scarlet fever that killed her father. But the fact that she survived, while her younger sister Maria did not, has led to suggestions that it might have been Strauss himself – given he was run down, depressed, generally unwell – who contracted the fever and passed it on to his children.

Early on the morning of 25 September, Anna Strauss, who it appears knew nothing of her ex-husband's illness, received news that he had died during the night. Her youngest son Eduard wrote many years later in strangely detached language that 'the poor deceased lay on wooden slats which had been taken from the bed and laid on the floor', and that Emilie had stripped the apartment in the Kumpfgasse of 'whatever could not be riveted or nailed firmly down'. A lengthy inventory of personal effects found in the apartment suggests this was at best an exaggeration.

Two days later members of Strauss's orchestra bore his coffin from the Kumpfgasse first to St Stephen's Cathedral for a funeral service, and from there to Döbling cemetery, where he was buried alongside his old friend and sometime foe, Joseph Lanner. A hundred thousand Viennese lined the funeral route.

The news was greeted with dismay in London. The *Illustrated London News* carried a lengthy obituary, in which it stated, 'Hosts of imitators have sprung up since Strauss, but to him will remain the glory of originality, fancy, feeling and invention.'

In Paris, Strauss's great admirer Hector Berlioz wrote his own tribute: 'Vienna without Strauss is like Austria without the Danube.'

Johann Strauss senior had led an extraordinary life. Born into comparative poverty in a tavern by the Danube, losing his father and mother tragically early, brought up by step-parents, he rose to be, in effect, an honorary member of the highest Viennese aristocracy. He had played before royalty and could number the likes of the Duke of Wellington, not to mention Queen Victoria, among his admirers.

His music, it is not an exaggeration to say, had changed Vienna for ever. It captured an era and achieved a popularity, not just in his home city but across Europe, that no other composer could equal.

But he had died, prematurely, at the age of forty-five. The way was now clear for his son, one month short of his twenty-fifth birthday, to take over where his father had left off. A young man spurred on by his father's opposition and intransigence, and who would go on to eclipse him totally.

Vienna now had just one Waltz King, one Johann Strauss.

Chapter 8

A New Waltz King

His reign as Vienna's new Waltz King did not begin easily for Johann Strauss the Younger. The would-be revolution of 1848 had failed and his past was catching up with him. There was a new emperor on the throne and the ruling classes had once more taken control, with the backing of the military.

Johann's overt sympathies for the firebrands counted against him. Things might have calmed down in Vienna, but the Austrian army was now fully stretched trying to quell a rebellion in Hungary. The survival of the Habsburg Empire itself was at stake, and with a new emperor on the throne this was no time to harbour republican sympathies.

To compound this, the elder Strauss's death unleashed a torrent of personal attacks on Johann. When he announced that he intended to take over his father's orchestra there was furious reaction, not least from the orchestral players themselves. What right did he, a young man of limited experience, have to assume the exalted position his father held? There was even a suggestion in some quarters that Johann's ruthlessness in pursuing his own career had hastened his father's premature death.

Johann was stung by the criticism and the force with which it had erupted, to such an extent that just eight days after his father's death he wrote what amounted to an extensive and heartfelt apologia in the mass-market *Wiener Zeitung*, appealing for sympathy and understanding of his circumstances: those of a young man struggling to make a career for himself against intractable opposition from an exalted musician who had broken up his family, yet to whom as a son he still felt deep love and loyalty:

> *Any son is to be pitied who weeps at the grave of his prematurely departed father; even more to be pitied, however, is one whose fate is determined by hostile elements of shattered family circumstances, who ... has to listen to judgement on himself and on those who have remained faithful to him from the strongly condemnatory mouths of his opponents, while he has no other weapon at his disposal other than to point to a deserted mother, and brothers and sisters who are not yet of age ... It was not a case, as hostile opponents have suggested, of entering into a prize fight with the far superior powers of the most skilful master of the craft, who was, at the same time, always my beloved*

father ... I chose the art for which I felt a vocation ... I only wish to earn the smallest part of the favour which my deserving father so richly reaped! ... and thus, at the same time, to fulfil my duty to my mother and my brothers and sisters.

It was a remarkable outpouring of emotion to lay before the wider newspaper-reading public. In fact, given Johann's character, it seems improbable that he would have gone into print in such a manner without a certain amount of advice from a quarter he respected.

That quarter is likely to have been the now ageing Franz Amon, the man who had secretly taught Johann the violin all those years ago and who still led the Johann Strauss Orchestra. As well as advising Johann to lay his emotions bare in public, he also reasoned with fellow members of the orchestra. What if they employed a new musical director and could no longer call themselves the Strauss Orchestra? Why throw a name away that was famous throughout Europe, when a younger member of the same family was exhibiting a talent and showmanship that might one day be as great as that of his father? What if the orchestra was to disband, and they were to find themselves without regular employment?

A combination of Johann's humility and Amon's diplomacy seems to have done the trick. We can surely discount the story that members of the orchestra presented Strauss's baton on a cushion to his son. What is fact, though, is that the 'Orchestra of the late Strauss' elected Johann its leader, and on 7 October 1849, in the Kolonadensaal of the Volksgarten, Johann stood for the first time at the head of his father's orchestra. If any doubters still needed to be won over, that was achieved by Johann's decision to devote the concert entirely to works by his father.

Yet Johann Strauss II's rehabilitation was not entirely complete. Resentment of his revolutionary sympathies still existed at the very highest level. His father's death had left vacant the prestigious post of Music Director of Imperial Court Balls. Johann put himself forward, but was rejected. It went instead, on the recommendation of the emperor's parents no less, to one Philipp Fahrbach.

Johann, ever one to trim his sails according to prevailing winds, composed a patriotic march designed to praise the emperor himself, *'Kaiser Franz Josef'*. Several other compositions were similarly designed to flatter. Yet it was to be a further eleven years before he was finally elevated to the position his father had held.

This did not prevent Johann performing in the very highest circles. When Emperor Franz Josef met the Russian tsar, Nikolai the First, during an autumn festival in Warsaw, it was Johann and the Strauss Orchestra who provided musical entertainment. And though he did not yet officially hold the title, Johann was invited to conduct at a charity ball in the Redoutensaal of the Hofburg Palace during the Carnival of 1851 – a sign of the gradual softening of official policy towards him.

In these early years after his father's death, Johann found himself again and again compared to his famous father, and often unfavourably. It is true that as yet, musically speaking, his compositions did not rank with those of the elder Strauss, though that was soon to change. But for flamboyance and flair, and sheer magnetism on the podium, swaying with his violin under his chin, he was every bit the equal of his father. His younger years, sparkling eyes, thick black hair, soon made him the undisputed darling of Vienna.

In another way too, he was his father's son. He seemed to have an endless capacity for sheer hard work. He was churning out compositions at an extraordinary rate. By the time of the 1851 Carnival he had the best part of a hundred compositions to his name, and he was not yet twenty-six years of age.

In constant demand, Johann was called on to organise engagements, compose new pieces, arrange others, rehearse the orchestra, and frequently conduct at several different venues on the same day. It was his father all over again, and the effect it had on him was very similar.

Despite his youth, his energy was not limitless. He soon paid the price. At the end of February 1851, four months after his twenty-fifth birthday, he suffered a collapse. He was reported in early March to be 'dangerously ill' from typhoid and 'nervous fever'. Amid a frenzy of speculation, one newspaper even reported the rumour that he had died.

In a further echo of his father, instead of convalescing he embarked on a concert trip to Germany, composing new pieces to take with him. This was soon followed by another concert tour through Prague, Leipzig, Berlin, Hamburg and Dresden.

Not surprisingly his health gave way again. This time it was more serious. He was unable to perform during the busy Christmas period of 1852. Several times, no doubt on his insistence, it was announced he was well enough to return to the podium, but each time it was postponed.

He did not return until six weeks later, and when he did it was characteristically with a vengeance. Two concerts back to back in different venues, with new compositions to premiere at each. When, on 18 February 1853, Emperor Franz Josef, strolling with a fellow officer on the Bastei, survived an assassination attempt – the sturdy high collar of his military uniform withstanding the knife of a Hungarian nationalist – Johann saw it as an opportunity to curry favour with the court, and composed his *'Kaiser Franz Josef I Rettungs-Jubel-Marsch'* ('March of Rejoicing at the Deliverance of Emperor Franz Josef I').*

In the post-Metternich era, under a new emperor, Vienna was celebrating a new freedom. New dance halls were

---

* The piece is typically upbeat, with the Austrian national anthem sitting unsubtly at its heart. There is no record of whether the emperor appreciated the gesture.

opening across the city, ever more grand and attracting more and more revellers. Johann and his orchestra were in demand everywhere. The rivalry with his father, the resentment towards him, were things of the past. Still from his father he retained one essential quality: the inability to say no.

Returning from a concert in the early hours of the morning, at the end of a day that had begun before dawn, Johann Strauss lost consciousness. This was followed by a nervous breakdown. At the age of twenty-seven he was very seriously ill.

This time there was no premature return to the podium. Johann's doctors ordered a prolonged stay at a sanatorium in Bad Gastein in the mountains south of Salzburg, followed by a further period of convalescence in Bad Neuhaus bei Cilli in south-east Austria.*

Crisis enveloped the Strauss family, the Strauss musical enterprise, in the Hirschenhaus. Step forward the matriarch of the family, Anna.

You can surely forgive Anna if she felt a certain amount of satisfaction, smugness even, in the way her family had turned out. She had been abandoned by her husband, her distress compounded by humiliation at her husband's open

---

* Today Slovenia.

acknowledgement of a second family, her finances always difficult, the overt opposition of her husband to their eldest son's musical ambitions, the sheer emotional pain and the practical difficulty of having an estranged, difficult, uncooperative husband living in the same house.

What had she achieved in the face of all that? She had raised three sons and two daughters single-handed. One was proving himself to be a master musician, at least as good as his father and possibly better. And who could claim credit for that? Who was it who ignored the father's opposition and arranged for secret violin lessons for the boy?

The second son, Josef, had qualified as a mechanical engineer, achieving first-class grades in technical drawing and mathematics, and was now making headway in his chosen profession of architecture. Eduard, the youngest, was showing an aptitude for music, becoming a skilled harpist. Both daughters were attractive, lively, bright young women, and she had every reason to hope they would settle into good marriages.

The tribulations she had suffered had instilled in Anna a driving ambition for her brood. Her eldest son Johann was undoubtedly the family breadwinner. It was the Johann Strauss Orchestra that not only supported the whole family but allowed them to remain in the large, comfortable Hirschenhaus and live a lifestyle worthy of the city's most famous musical dynasty.

Now, for the first time since her husband's untimely – but probably not too unwelcome – death, the family enterprise was under threat. The new head of the household, the man on whom their continued existence depended, had succumbed to a debilitating illness, which had put him out of action.

Something needed to be done, and quickly. Anna knew what was called for. She discussed it with Johann, and he was in full agreement. It is possible he had already reached the same conclusion himself. The family business of music could not be allowed to falter. It needed someone new at its head, someone familiar with its ways, someone who could be relied on and trusted. It did not need at this stage to be permanent, but it would serve until Johann was fully recovered and could resume his duties.

The choice of person was obvious. Who knew Johann and his ways better than anyone? Who understood the tensions and difficulties that existed in the Hirschenhaus more intimately than any other? Who would have the interests of the family closest to his heart?

Josef Strauss the nascent architect. A Strauss himself. Anna and Johann laid out the situation before him. The future of the family, the future of the Johann Strauss Orchestra, lay in his hands. He needed to step forward and ensure the family's wellbeing.

The only problem was that Josef had never shown any interest in music. He was an engineer and would-be architect, not a musician. The family's musical business would have to get along without him.

He said no.

Chapter 9

'Pepi' Joins the Family Firm

Josef was used to his own wishes being discounted by the family. Just as Strauss senior had tried to prevent his eldest son from pursuing a career in music, so he had early plans for Josef to enter the military. Josef reacted furiously, at the age of twenty-one banging off an angry letter to his father:

> Leave me where I am; leave me what I am; don't snatch me away from a life that can bring me so many joys ... Do not cast me into that rough, inconsistent world which destroys all feeling for humanity, a world for which I am not fitted, to which I was not born ... I do not want to learn to kill people ... I want to serve mankind as a human being ...

That letter pretty much summed up Josef, apart from the anger. He had a shy, gentle character, he was universally liked and content to make his own way in life without interference or influence from outside.

He had his way over his father, though less from the force of his argument than the fact that Strauss senior was about to leave on an extensive tour lasting the best part of a year and died shortly after his return.

Now, in 1853, as his elder brother lay ill on sick leave, Josef was attending courses on hydraulic engineering and water-works construction to work towards a diploma in engineering. In May he established his reputation as an innovative engineer by designing, with a colleague, a horse-drawn street-cleaning machine with rotating brushes. At first rejected as impractical, the Vienna Municipal Council later realised its worth and the plans went into production.[*]

A quietly satisfied Josef began work on a snow-clearing machine, which was when his mother and elder brother told him they had other plans for him. He was needed as part of the Strauss musical enterprise. Josef was quietly defiant. He had seen his father off over plans to enter the military; he would do the same now.

Except that Anna and Johann knew exactly how to handle Josef: to appeal to his better nature, to explain to him that the welfare of the whole family – mother, brothers and sisters – depended on him, how they all looked to him to

---

[*] Apart from obvious advances in technology, the basic design remains largely unchanged to this day.

save them from destitution. As a clinching argument they stressed that it would be only a temporary arrangement, until Johann regained his health.

Josef could fight his uncaring father, but had no weaponry against his loved ones, those nearest and dearest to him. To the childhood friend he would marry in five years' time, Karoline Josefa Pruckmayer, he wrote on 23 July 1853, 'The unavoidable has happened; today I play for the first time at the Sperl ... I wholeheartedly regret that this has happened so suddenly.'

'Suddenly' is the operative word. It had all happened so quickly that Josef had no time to become even passably efficient on the violin, so that he had to conduct at the Sperl with a baton – a severe break with Strauss tradition.

With characteristic dedication he took lessons in the violin and conducting, and even set about composing, mindful that each Strauss concert contained new pieces composed specially for the occasion.

The arts were not entirely alien to this talented engineer. For several years he had complemented his courses at the Polytechnic Institute with private tuition in drawing and painting at the Academy of Fine Arts. He had turned out many drawings, silhouettes, watercolours, all exhibiting great finesse and detail. He was accomplished in the literary field as well. He had written an anthology of poems, and an ambitious drama in five acts for which he wrote the text, visualised the settings and produced sketches of the characters, costumes and scenery.

By all accounts Josef – 'Pepi' to close friends and family – was a shy, sensitive man. The relatively few photographs of him show a gentle, almost soft, countenance, albeit with a firm gaze, prominent chin, and a characteristically Straussian full and flowing head of hair. He felt strongly enough about the upheavals of 1848 to join the Student Legion, even possessing guns, and at one point found himself the subject of an arrest warrant.

This seems to have been a passing phase, or rather a good example of that Viennese dual nature, crying on one side of the face and laughing on the other. A journalist described Josef as 'so audaciously stylish, so high-spiritedly Viennese when in cheerful company, and so artistically dreamy in the realm of music'.

We have no first-hand accounts of his debut with the Johann Strauss Orchestra at the Sperl, but he was soon booked to appear again – or, more accurately, had no choice but to fulfil his brother's next engagement, which was for the Parish Festival Ball in the Viennese suburb of Hernals on 29 August 1853.

This was the moment to find out if he had any talent at composing – I suspect as much for himself as for the orchestra and audience. He composed a piece to which he gave the opus number 1, and chose a title that intentionally left no one in any doubt that this was a temporary departure from his chosen career.

Die Ersten und Letzten' ('The First and Last') is an extraordinary first work for a trained engineer in his mid-twenties. It begins with an uncharacteristically bold fanfare, for a shy man, repeated several times just in case you missed it. A slow introduction follows, a pause, and then comes a truly delightful passage in three-four time, followed by another. We are unmistakably in Strauss territory. This is music to sway to, swing a wine glass or beer jug to. It is a substantial piece, lasting around ten minutes, and ends with a typical Straussian *accelerando*, a roll on the side-drum and a flourish to finish.

Josef Strauss might have been a reluctant musician, but he had arrived and there was no turning back. The theatrical journal *Bäuerle's Theaterzeitung* reported that *'Die Ersten und Letzten'* was repeated six times at the request of the crowd, and just in case Josef had any doubts about his future in music, it wrote with clear reference to the title:

> *This latest flowering of the dance is positive proof of the brilliant talent of Herr Strauss, and we allow ourselves the agreeable hope that this composition will not be the last, but that Josef Strauss … will soon produce a sequel.*

Josef Strauss did more than that. In less than two decades he was to compose more than three hundred pieces and arrange at least five hundred others. To this day musicologists argue that Josef was, generally speaking, a finer orchestrator than his brother, and that his best waltzes – *'Sphären-Klänge'* ('Sounds of the Spheres'), *'Dorfschwalben aus Österreich'* ('Village Swallows of Austria') – are as good, if not better, than Johann's best.

Johann himself would later be in no doubt. 'Pepi is the more gifted of us two; I am merely the more popular,' he would say.

Josef's musical life flourished along with the family enterprise he helped save. It is fair to say, though, that he was not as temperamentally suited to it as his elder brother, and his career was to come to a sudden and tragic end.

Johann Strauss returned to Vienna on 18 September 1853, 'completely restored after his illness', and within a very short time he received an offer he could not refuse. The Johann Strauss Orchestra, with Johann once again at its head, was about to become truly international.

Several hundred miles to the north-east of Vienna, Russia had proudly opened its first railway, a short nineteen-mile stretch linking the capital of St Petersburg with the town of Pavlovsk, a favourite summer resort of the tsar and the nobility. There an elegant music pavilion had been constructed at the railway terminus and named the Vauxhall Pavilion, after the famous pleasure gardens in London.*

---

* Thus giving the word *vokzal*, meaning central railway station, to the Russian language.

This had happened in 1837 and in the intervening years prominent musicians had been invited from across Europe to perform there for the distinguished visitors to Pavlosk. Franz Liszt and Robert and Clara Schumann had all played there, and the railway management had attempted to persuade Johann Strauss senior and his orchestra to visit Pavlovsk in 1839, but without success.

The railway company was now under new management and it was time to try again to entice the most famous orchestral leader in Europe to travel to Pavlovsk – if not the father, then this time the son. Accordingly, in 1854 the new director of the Tsarskoye-Selo Railway Company led a delegation to see Johann Strauss the Younger.

The offer on the table was an invitation to conduct the summer concerts at Pavlovsk two years hence, in 1856. To keep costs down it was proposed that Johann make use of local musicians.

How could he possibly say no to this? An invitation to the imperial capital of Russia, to perform before the *crème de la crème* of Russian aristocracy, including most probably the tsar himself and his tsarina. If he could make a success of this, his name would truly be established internationally.

But Johann was worried on two counts. First, there was the problem that he would be working with musicians unused to playing his music, compounded by language difficulties. Secondly, and rather more concerning, were the reservations he had about leaving the Johann Strauss Orchestra in the hands of brother Josef in Vienna.

Josef had shown he could conduct and compose, but in these early and critical years was his heart really in a musical career? Johann was not sure. Fickle as the musical world was, he knew it would take only one or two poor concerts and the reputation of the orchestra could be irretrievably damaged.

It is at this point that the third Strauss brother, Eduard, enters the story. He was nearly ten years younger than Johann and almost eight younger than Josef. There is scant information on Eduard's early years. Too young to have become politically active during the 1848 uprising, and with his father so often away on tour and at home with his mistress when he was in Vienna, it is unlikely that Eduard was able to develop a close relationship with him. Strauss senior died when Eduard was just fourteen.

Given this, I think we can also assume that Strauss senior was too uninterested and distracted to bother trying to dissuade his youngest son from a career in music, for this – remarkably – is what Eduard seems to have pursued. Anna must have been incredulous when it became obvious to her that Eduard, like his brothers, was extraordinarily gifted musically. All three sons, each of them highly talented musicians from an early age. Anna had had her revenge on her husband three times over!

In 1855, at the age of twenty, Eduard was playing harp in the Johann Strauss Orchestra. Vienna was now growing accustomed to seeing the three Strauss brothers all involved in the same enterprise, often appearing at the same venue together – or at least two out of the three – deputising for each other, and generally running light-music activities at the city's dance halls.

The Strausses – all three of them – were on the musical map, and it became obvious to them, and the people of Vienna, that they would never leave it. It was at about this time that Johann took to adopting the French version of his name, Jean.* Josef, as we have seen, was known as Pepi, and Eduard as Edi — later 'der schöne Edi' ('beautiful Edi') due to his good looks, coupled with a fondness for smart clothes and fashion.

With his two brothers now involved with the orchestra, Johann overcame his earlier doubts regarding Josef's commitment and accepted the invitation to Russia. The first concert at Pavlovsk was the best part of two years away, which would give him time to prepare and make sure that all was in place in Vienna before he left.

In the event the invitation to Russia was to prove far more of a commitment than he could possibly have imagined. It was to change his life, and not just musically. He would – as far as we know, for the first time – fall head over heels in love.

---

* He was not alone among composers for adopting more exotic forms of their names. Beethoven was fond of signing manuscripts and letters Louis or Luigi van Beethoven.

Chapter 10

In Russia and in Love

To say that the concerts went well in the summer of 1856 would be an understatement of huge proportions. At the opening concert in Pavlovsk on 18 May, which included pieces by Strauss father and son, as well as Verdi and Meyerbeer, there were so many demands for repeats and encores that the concert lasted until 1 a.m.

Word quickly spread. The aristocracy of St Petersburg made the train journey to Pavlovsk several times a week. It was soon impossible to get tickets at any price for a Strauss concert. It was reported that more than once, when a bell was sounded to announce the departure of the last train to the capital, the audience paid no attention, refusing to allow Strauss to stop, knowing it would mean camping down somewhere for the night away from home.

It was only a matter of time before the tsar himself, accompanied by members of the royal family, took their places in the imperial box. Once the tsar was seen to clap enthusiastically, there was not a single personage who did not follow his example. Johann Strauss, idol of Vienna, was soon known and lauded throughout Russia west of the Urals. His fame was truly international.

Hardly surprisingly, in the autumn of 1856 Strauss was signed up for the following two years. The demands on him were quite extraordinary. He was to give daily concerts from 2 May to 2 October with an orchestra of not less than thirty musicians. Daily concerts for five months – it's a schedule that would cause any of today's globe-trotting maestros or virtuosos to blanch. In fact it's unlikely any would agree to such a punishing schedule.

Nor was he totally free to select the music. He was to choose pieces from classical opera as well as garden and dance music, but 'in this he is to follow the taste of the local audience'. He would be expected to feature his own compositions, but 'he is also to perform the most popular and latest compositions of other famous masters, with a full orchestra under his personal direction'.

The remuneration, on the other hand, was exceedingly generous. He received 18,000 silver roubles for the five-month engagement each year, including his own and his orchestra's wages and travel costs.* He and his players also received free accommodation, and were permitted to give four benefit concerts each season, meaning all proceeds accrued to Strauss and the orchestra.

---

* Around £90,000–£100,000 in today's money.

In the first season he had accepted the offer of local musicians to keep costs down, but this new contract required him to organise his own orchestra. It's possible Strauss himself insisted on this to ensure the players were up to scratch. In this he most certainly succeeded. He brought just a nucleus of musicians from Vienna, supplementing them with hand-picked players from Berlin to reduce costs, as the journey from Berlin was direct and therefore cheaper. It was a good move. In May 1857 he wrote to his music publisher in Vienna, 'My orchestra is causing a sensation, and they deserve it too, for would to God I had such a band in Vienna. I cannot speak *too highly* of this one ...'

A 'sensation' the Strauss Orchestra most certainly was. The initial single-year contract, as we have seen, was extended for a further two years. In the event Johann Strauss was to appear with his orchestra in Pavlovsk every summer for almost a decade, from 1856 to 1865, and again in 1869 and considerably later in 1886.

The Russian nobility was almost as familiar with Johann Strauss and his orchestra as were the concertgoers of Vienna. In some senses even more so. Two of Tsar Alexander's brothers were accomplished cellists. Both asked if they could sit in and play with the orchestra. Strauss readily agreed.

The 'Russian summers' produced some of Strauss's best-loved works, many of which received their first performance in Pavlosk, among them *'Pizzicato-Polka'*,

'Champagner-Polka', and *'Krönungs-Marsch'* (dedicated to Tsar Alexander II on his coronation in Moscow).

One work, *'Bauern-Polka'* ('Peasants' Polka'), a catchy, instantly memorable little piece with vocal refrain, was more than a success. One report accorded it the ultimate accolade. The piece 'brought a storm of applause such as no movement from a Beethoven symphony could yet have received'. It was demanded over and over again by so many audiences that Strauss himself was apparently driven to distraction.*

One other composition deserves particular attention. It remains to this day one of his best-known and most often performed pieces and its origin is, to say the least, interesting.

It is hardly surprising, given not just his celebrity, his extraordinary musical talent, but also his extreme good looks – dark lustrous hair, swarthy skin and blazing eyes, an eye for fashion and always immaculately turned out – that Johann Strauss was a magnet for Russian women. It soon became *de rigueur* for the ladies to vie for his attention by brandishing cigarette packets that bore his portrait and autograph.

Word quickly spread back to Vienna, where rumours abounded of 'Dashing Jean's' amorous relationships in

---

* The *'Bauern-Polka'* is a favourite at the Vienna New Year's Day concert to this day, with the vocal refrain *'La-la-la-laa'* traditionally provided by the unsmiling members of the Vienna Philharmonic Orchestra. Perhaps it was a similar rendition by the Strauss Orchestra in Pavlovsk that made it such a favourite.

Russia. These were soon picked up by the satirical journal *Tritsch-Tratsch* ('Gossip, or Tittle-Tattle'). The truth, or otherwise, of these rumours is impossible to ascertain at a distance of more than a century and a half, but it remains a fact that Strauss dashed off a lively little polka which he entitled '*Tritsch-Tratsch*'.

Did he compose it as a riposte to the rumours being printed about him, or even a subtle endorsement? Either is possible, given his willingness to compose new pieces relating to current events. Whatever the truth of the rumours, Strauss was a single man and they cannot have hurt his reputation.

Certainly back in Vienna the coincidence will not have gone unnoticed. Indeed it was in Vienna, not Pavlovsk, that the piece was first performed. It was an instant sensation. One reviewer wrote, with possibly a hint of *double-entendre*, 'Seemingly no dance composition of such freshness, humorous colouring, and spicy instrumentation has been published in years.' The piano sheet music sold out practically overnight.

Whether or not the reports of amorous affairs were true, there is one that most certainly happened. Her name was Olga Smirnitzky.

Exactly how Strauss met Olga we do not know, but it seems the two came to know each other in 1858, Strauss's third year in Pavlovsk. Olga was twenty years of age, Strauss thirteen years her senior. She was musically gifted and the daughter of aristocratic Russian parents. Intelligent, well read, able to converse in French, she was also 'romantic, sentimental, with a sense of humour and tantalising moods', according to a friend of the family.

Of those qualities it was 'tantalising' that most made its mark on the impressionable Strauss. He nicknamed her 'L'Espiègle' ('The Mischievous One') and was later to compose a piece he called *'L'Espiègle'*, published in Vienna as *'Der Kobold'* ('The Imp'), with a theme as flighty and unpredictable as the woman it depicts. But there is a core of steel running through the piece, and it ends with firm and final chords – an accurate depiction not just of Olga, but of their relationship too.

Johann Strauss, famous throughout Europe, lauded wherever he went, surrounded by admirers and sycophants of both sexes, fell hopelessly in love with Olga. He took to writing her heartfelt and passionate letters, often late at night after a concert.

'I am more and more convinced', he wrote on 21 July, 'that you are the being destined for me by God, and there is no space within me which could harbour the thought of living without you – Jean.'

After a concert in which he had played Schumann, he wrote:

Even before the concert I was hopelessly enveloped in melancholy and this was increased to a supreme pitch

by Schumann's music ... Why can I not be like other
people? Olga, how unhappy I am! I have never wept
for myself before, but today – I could confess it to no
one but you – it happened.

As for Olga, she seemed to relish the obvious power she had
over such a famous individual. She was clearly not above
taunting him, judging by one note he wrote to her: 'If you
see me suffer, why not tear my heart out completely with
just one scornful glance?' In another he wrote, 'Naughty
little child, why did you scold me so?'

The two clearly took great pains to keep their relationship secret, but Olga's parents were keeping a close eye
on their daughter, and they did not like what they saw.
The family was aristocratic, moving in the highest circles,
wealthy and landed, and a match with a mere musician
simply was not on the cards. Even a musician with his own
orchestra, whose autographed picture they will have seen
on sale for 10 kopeks at every station in St Petersburg. A
musician was still a musician, and a musician was no catch
for their daughter.

It appears it was Olga's mother who wore the trousers. On a day in September she summoned Strauss to the
sumptuous Smirnitzky *palais*. One can imagine he set off
in high spirits, relishing the opportunity to get to know the
woman better who, if things went according to plan, might
one day be his mother-in-law.

But if that was his plan, he was soon disabused of the

notion. Olga's mother left him in no doubt that she and her husband disapproved of the relationship and they were putting an end to it. She went further, stunning Strauss with bitter invective against her own daughter, describing her as meaning not a word of what she said, even of being inspired by the devil.

Strauss, badly shaken, sent Olga a note saying he had quickly come to hate a mother 'who could say such insulting things about her own child'. He went on, 'Her behaviour to me was heartless and indelicate.' He told Olga her mother had demanded he hand over all her letters to him, 'but I swore to her that your letters were to accompany me to my grave … that I need those letters to preserve my own life and I cannot do without them.'

It appears Olga was prepared to side with her paramour to some extent, at least initially. She sent him further notes expressing her love, but the notes soon stopped altogether.

Strauss left Pavlovsk an unhappy man, but he had other things on his mind. He had to conduct a concert in honour of the centenary of the birth of Friedrich Schiller on 10 November.

He threw himself into his work, but there were distractions. He was no doubt upset to find that his relationship with Olga was common knowledge in Vienna, and there must have been knowing looks, whispers behind the hand at his concerts, even in the street. Was it also known that he had been seen off by the girl's mother, that he had been in effect humiliated?

Stories were told at his expense. One rumour circulated that after a concert a woman approached him and whispered in his ear, 'If only my name was Olga.' Whether that was true or not, it is certain Strauss was aware of what wagging tongues were saying.

They were wagging closer to home too. It was widely believed matriarch Anna gave her eldest son a stern talking to, telling him to pull himself together. His brothers are certain to have taken the lead from their mother and given Johann some fraternal ribbing. For a man in his early thirties, criticism, even derision, from those closest to him might have been the most difficult to bear of all.

Johann Strauss was an artist, with an artist's sensibilities. He had been hurt; now he needed to get over it. In this painful task he received help from a totally unexpected source – Olga herself.

In the spring of 1860 a letter arrived in Vienna for Strauss. It was from Olga.

> *Do not condemn me when you read these lines. I will be brief and not embark on long explanation. I have been engaged for two weeks … Forget your unfaithful imp.*

And forget her he did. He returned for many more years to Pavlovsk, but there were no painful reunions, no secret meetings, no regrets. Olga Smirnitzky had dropped completely out of Johann Strauss's life.

But Strauss was not finished with love. At around the time he was pining for Olga in Vienna he was introduced to a singer renowned for her fine mezzo-soprano voice. Her name was Henriette Chalupetzky. It is possible, given her musical reputation and the frequency of her appearances on stage, that he made her acquaintance some years earlier. But it was only in the winter of 1861–2 that the relationship become something deeper.

It was as unlikely a liaison as that with Olga, although for very different reasons. Henriette was lauded for her performances across Europe, some critics even comparing her favourably with the Swedish Nightingale, the soprano Jenny Lind. Mendelssohn and Berlioz, no less, had dedicated songs to her.

But at a remarkably young age, somewhere in her early to mid-twenties, and already considerably wealthy, she gave it all up for an entirely different life – a somewhat colourful life, to put it mildly. It's believed that in her twenties she bore no fewer than seven illegitimate children, the paternity of only two of whom is known.

At the age of twenty-five or thereabouts she became the mistress of the banker Moritz Todesco, a patron of the arts whose sumptuous house on the newly opened Ringstrasse abounded with artists, writers, musicians. It was there that Henriette played hostess to salon soirées, the baron's wife Sofie apparently complicit, willingly or otherwise.

If Henriette had ambitions to replace Sofie as baroness, she was to be disappointed. The baron was Jewish, Henriette Roman Catholic, and the law forbade persons of different religions to marry. Henriette was clearly not too upset though, since she remained Baron Todesco's mistress for a full eighteen years. Two of her children were his.

Then she met the most famous musician in Vienna, a friendship formed, and at some point it became intimate. They were in love, and Johann Strauss asked her to marry him. She was, technically, a free woman. The only potential problem was her relationship with the baron, but that proved not to be a problem at all. He understood entirely her nature, her artistic passion, and he consented totally to release her. He even consented to Henriette's request that he should keep custody of their two daughters so they could take his aristocratic title, allowing her access to them whenever she wished.

Henriette was free to marry Strauss. The path to marriage was not entirely smooth, however. Henriette's lifestyle was well known: her role as mistress, her illegitimate children, even her professional life as a singer was not regarded as an entirely wholesome career for a woman to pursue. Strauss encountered family opposition, most vocally from Josef, who was standing in for his elder brother in Pavlovsk when Johann announced his engagement. The quiet, reluctant musician conceded that Henriette was 'very well preserved', but knew of her reputation, adding that at forty-four she was seven years older than Johann. Matriarch Anna probably allowed herself to be persuaded by the fact that Henriette had a considerable fortune of her own, and was hardly likely to be a 'gold-digger'.

On 27 August 1862, in St Stephen's Cathedral in the heart of Vienna, Johann Strauss, 'Kapellmeister und Musikdirektor', married Henriette Chalupetzky, 'of single status'.

But Henriette Chalupetzky is not the name by which Strauss's bride is known to history. Early in her singing career she adopted the more exotic name of Jetty Treffz – the same Jetty Treffz who thirteen years earlier had shared the stage at London's Exeter Hall with Johann Strauss senior. What might he have thought then had he known that the singer on stage with him would one day marry his eldest son, making him her father-in-law?

Jetty Treffz was now Jetty Strauss. Johann Strauss the Younger, just two months short of his thirty-eighth birthday, was a married man. The extraordinary thing is that despite Jetty's exotic and uncertain past, despite the difference in age, despite family opposition and everything that seemed to mitigate against the marriage working, Johann Strauss could not have chosen a more suitable wife.

Chapter 11

Tying the Knot

Another, more historically significant, wedding had taken place in Vienna eight years earlier. It united two people totally unsuited to each other, temperamentally, emotionally, and even as first cousins genetically. It was a marriage that would be critically damaged by misunderstandings, divergent interests, absences and separation, and wounded beyond repair by suicide and murder.

On 24 April 1854, in St Augustine's Church alongside the imperial Hofburg Palace, Emperor Franz Josef married Elisabeth of Bavaria, known to history as Sisi. The emperor's accession to the imperial throne as a young man of eighteen, following the street revolution of 1848 and the enforced departure of Chancellor Metternich, ushered in a new era in every sense in Vienna.

A city that had been more or less in shutdown for more than thirty years revelled in its newfound gaiety. At last people could talk openly in the street, in cafés and in the back of horse-drawn cabs;[*] spies were a thing of the past; it was safe to go out at night; new dance halls opened and flourished; the waltz shook off any suspicion and the music of the Strauss family swept the city. Metternich was gone, there was a new young emperor on the throne. The refuge sought in cosy domesticity during the Biedermeier era was no longer required.

It was, admittedly, an earlier emperor who, responding to a proposal to construct licensed brothels, replied, 'The walls would cost me nothing, but the expense of roofing would be ruinous, for it would be necessary to put a roof over the whole city,' but it might have applied just as aptly as Vienna entered the second half of the nineteenth century, and with considerably more openness.

The single most potent symbol of a new era dawning came about as a result of an order by the new emperor that the Bastei should be pulled down and replaced by a wide boulevard encircling the city.

This massive, metres-thick, city wall – so wide that a spacious walkway on top provided a fashionable area for people to stroll along, and for jugglers and street entertainers to ply their trade; so impenetrable that gates set into it at regular distances provided the only points at which it could be passed through – had been built nearly three centuries before, following the first Turkish invasion in 1529.

---

* Known then and now as 'fiacres'.

Now not only had the threat from the Ottoman empire dissipated, but Vienna was witnessing the most rapid expansion in its history. In under a decade in the mid-nineteenth century the population soared by 30 per cent. The city was spreading well beyond the city wall. Where once a few carriages might have clattered along rarely frequented alleys, now there was all the bustle of a burgeoning city.

The Bastei had done its job. It had to go, and so Emperor Franz Josef – well aware he was upsetting the traditionalists – ordered its demolition. It was to be the largest building project in Vienna's history, turning the imperial capital into a vast building site. It was carried out carefully and painstakingly. Experts had to calculate exactly the right amount of explosives to demolish the wall, and not vast areas of the inner city with it.

In one way or another – a new building here or another one there – the work took more than two decades. But the all-important task, the demolition of the Bastei itself, symbol of Vienna's past, took seven years. On 1 May 1865 the emperor and his empress rode in a ceremonial carriage along the new boulevard (or at least that part of it that was complete) and officially declared it open.

The Ringstrasse, as it was named then and still is today, would come to encircle the inner city of Vienna. It soon became nearly two hundred feet wide, comprising a broad central section for carriages and later vehicles, flanked by two tree-shaded lanes for horse riders, and ample pathways for promenaders under double rows of trees.

The city's largest and most imposing buildings began to be sited along the Ringstrasse. The first of these was the Opera House, soon followed by the Parliament building, the City Hall, the Stock Exchange, the Imperial Theatre.*

Vienna was changing. It was entering a new era, and there was no going back.

This was the Vienna in which Johann Strauss was making his name. His music – and to a lesser extent that of his brothers – symbolised the new era. It also encapsulated the mood of the Viennese, celebrating their liberty, their new ruler, a newly thriving economy. There was employment to be had, and when a day's work was done, what better entertainment than to go to one of the dance halls, eat and drink, and dance to Strauss?

As for the composer, demand for his music – and for the man himself – was so huge he simply could not keep up with it. He needed to make changes in order to cope. On 5 February 1861 it was announced: 'For the first time in Vienna. THREE BALLS IN ONE EVENING. Three large orchestras.'

Each one was a Strauss orchestra. How was this to be done? Johann took the decision to elevate his youngest

---

* To this day the Ringstrasse holds the most important buildings of government, the largest hotels, the most imposing shops.

brother Eduard to the podium. Each of the three brothers was now conducting a Strauss orchestra.

Still the toll on Johann was heavy. He was not just the most prolific composer: essentially he was running the whole enterprise. He also knew he was the one the audiences wanted to see. In 1862, preparing to leave for his seventh season in Pavlovsk, he received an offer to appear in Paris with his orchestra for three consecutive years for an annual fee of 100,000 francs. The work would simply not stop coming in. He turned it down, which just a few years earlier would have been unthinkable.

While in Pavlovsk Johann Strauss fell ill again. It was an intermittent ailment and the doctors did not make a diagnosis. Strauss handed conducting duties over to a deputy, to the disappointment of audiences. In July he wired home for Eduard to take over from him. Anna intervened and insisted Josef should go instead.

Josef was angry. A reluctant musician in the first place, he objected to having his life disrupted at the whim of his elder brother. Once in Pavlovsk, and sharing conducting duties with Johann on the first night, he was resentful and deeply suspicious. On the morning Johann left for home, Josef wrote to his wife, 'He was more fresh and healthy than ever before. This time he has fooled physicians, doctors, everybody.'

He might well have been right. Strauss was clearly tired, if not close to exhaustion, but fundamentally it seems there was nothing wrong with him. Exactly three weeks after leaving Russia, Johann Strauss was well enough to marry Jetty Treffz.

The newest member of the Strauss family now proved herself to be not just a deeply caring wife, but also a highly efficient organiser. As one modern biographer puts it, Jetty became the complete companion for her husband – 'wife, lover, artistic adviser, private secretary, organiser, music-copyist, and even [as we shall see] nurse'.*

Jetty quickly saw that it was the conducting engagements that drained her husband most, not just the constant late nights but the extraordinary physical demands, given the way Johann threw himself into leading the orchestra from the violin.

As early as their honeymoon in Venice she tried to get him to relax, to have 'a complete rest' as she wrote to a friend. He did not entirely obey, composing the waltz *'Carnavals-Botschafter'* ('Carnival's Ambassador') and also – possibly to placate her – the delightful little *'Bluette, Polka française'*, which he dedicated to her.

Once back in Vienna, Jetty to all intents and purposes took over the running of the Strauss family enterprise. Her mother-in-law, now in her sixties and in the final decade of her life, was content to relinquish any remaining duties, and Jetty took over the organisation of concert tours, as well as contracts with performance venues.

As an artist herself, she had an innate understanding

---

* Peter Kemp, *The Strauss Family*, Omnibus Press, 1989.

of the world in which Johann operated, and unlike many artists (then and now) she also had a keen business sense, certainly better than her husband's. Johann, recognising this, was content to leave all financial matters in her hands.

Jetty also insisted on a move out of the family home. She chose an apartment that was close to the Hirschenhaus, recognising the need for Johann to be near to the family, but not smothered by it. In the following two years Johann and Jetty moved twice more, as she got a grip on the finances and their situation improved.

She also made a determined effort to right a past wrong, which she knew would lift her husband's self-esteem beyond measure. Twice before, in 1856 and 1859, Strauss had applied for the coveted post of Imperial Music Director and was turned down both times. A secret police report in 1856, nearly a decade after the street revolution, described him in extraordinary terms as 'a reckless, improper and profligate person', as though he could not escape his past activities and allegiances.

Now, on 20 February 1863, he applied for a third time at his wife's urging. One can almost imagine Jetty standing over him as he wrote the application. Five days later he was awarded the honorary title by decree, which noted that his questionable civil and moral behaviour of the past had now been mitigated by his 'many artistic, patriotic and charitable' accomplishments.

Strauss had left his political past, with its brief flirtation with revolution, firmly behind. He was now a true Establishment figure.

Jetty continued to cement her hold on the family enterprise, with the well-being of her husband at the forefront of her plans. She decreed that from now on Johann was only to conduct in exceptional circumstances. He was no longer to have permanent contracts with the owners of dance halls. Conducting duties were to be taken over by Josef and Eduard, to allow Johann time and energy for composing.

If Jetty's actions might be expected to cause any tension in the family, the opposite was the case. Josef had by now reconciled himself to being an indispensable part of the family enterprise, and had certainly reversed his earlier misgivings about Jetty's suitability as Johann's wife.

When one summer Jetty accompanied Johann and Josef to Pavlovsk, Josef wrote home to his wife:

> *Jetty is indispensable. She writes up all the accounts, copies out orchestral parts, sees to everything in the kitchen, and looks after everything with an efficiency and kindness that is admirable.*

Jetty was most certainly happy too. In Pavlovsk (though not as far as we know in Vienna) she gave a number of song recitals, and she wrote to a friend:

> *I am the happiest of wives, enjoying an idyllic life with my Jeany-boy ... who has made life seem desirable to*

*me again after it had become loathesome and a torment
to me.*

Her 'Jeany-boy' was now seriously wealthy. Jetty had
brought her own considerable earnings to the marriage,
and under her supervision her husband was commanding
huge fees.

Johann Strauss had long harboured ambitions to own
a house of his own. With Jetty in charge of finances, he
was able to fulfil that desire after just five years of marriage.
During 1868 the couple bought a house in the most stylish
suburb of Vienna, Hietzing, directly opposite the botanical
garden of Schönbrunn, part of the palace itself, with views
to the west of the hills of the Vienna woods and to the
north the city itself with the spire of St Stephen's Cathedral
rising from its centre.

It was a two-storey mansion, which Jetty was to fur-
nish in elaborate style, and one can forgive her a touch
of *lèse-majesté* in her description of it, written in October
1868:

> *Johann has bought a small house here, so really nice
> and comfortable that we imagine we are living in dear
> Albion [England]. Opposite us is the Schönbrunn bo-
> tanical garden, and the inside of our house is lovely.*

Even before the move, in a happy marriage with onerous
duties lifted from his shoulders, Strauss's creative juices

were flowing. The magnificent *'Geschichten aus dem Wienerwald'* ('Tales from the Vienna Woods') dates from this period, with its famous solo on Austria's national instrument, the zither.

Not long before, he had also composed what could be said to be his first truly great waltz, *'Morgenblätter'* ('Morning Papers'), all the more extraordinary when you consider he gave it the opus number 279 – in other words nearly 300 pieces already composed, and literally hundreds more still to come.*

'Morgenblätter' was written to a commission from the organising committee of the Concordia Ball, which was staged annually by a society of Austrian journalists (and given its appropriate title by them).

Strauss received another commission at around this time, from the Wiener Männergesang-Verein (Vienna Men's Chorus). It is slightly surprising that Strauss accepted the commission, given the fate of his last commission from them. It was good that he did so, however, as it resulted in another of Strauss's best waltzes, *'Wein, Weib und Gesang!'* ('Wine, Woman and Song!').†

The slightly earlier commission has an interesting history. The society asked Strauss to compose a choral work for them. Strauss accepted, despite the fact he was unused

---

* This is arguably the largest output of quality pieces in the history of classical music, possibly equalled only by the German Baroque composer Telemann.

† The exclamation mark is a particularly Straussian touch.

to writing for voices. Maybe he relished the challenge. Maybe Jetty did not, because for the best part of two years he did nothing about it.

He finally produced a new waltz for them for unaccompanied voices – actually four waltz numbers with introduction and brief coda – using words written by one of the chorus members, who fancied himself a poet. He then sent a hastily written piano accompaniment, with a note of apology: 'Please excuse the poor and untidy handwriting – I was obliged to get it finished within a few minutes. Johann Strauss.' (Is it too fanciful to imagine him scribbling this note down quickly while Jetty was out of the room?) Even closer to the first performance he provided an orchestral accompaniment.

Strauss was not present when the men's choir performed it, having conducting duties elsewhere, but was said to be seriously disappointed at its apparently poor reception. Actually several newspaper critics wrote the next day that the piece was 'splendid', 'catchy', 'lovely'. But it is surely a measure of just how popular Strauss's music was that the fact that the choral piece received just a single encore amounted to a failure.

Strauss put it to one side with a shrug, apparently saying to Josef, 'To hell with the waltz. I am only sorry about the coda. I thought that would be a success.'

More important matters loomed. Strauss had been invited to the most cosmopolitan, exciting, lively city in Continental Europe. His father might have performed in

Paris thirty years earlier, but Johann Strauss the Younger never had. In the summer of 1867 that changed.

The Paris engagement did not begin well. In the first place Strauss had to engage an entirely new orchestra, since his own had commitments in Vienna. Secondly there were general complaints that Strauss played the waltz too quickly, making it difficult to dance to. Most detrimental of all, Paris was staging a World Exhibition: Strauss was merely one of many attractions.

Everything changed when the newspaper *Le Figaro* not only praised Strauss and his music, but began to champion it and recommend it day after day. It had the desired effect. Jetty was soon able to write home:

> *The receipts have increased every day and the public is so frantically aflame for Jean that I cannot find words to depict this enthusiasm … they are simply crazy for this Viennese music.*

Strauss was suddenly in such demand that he had to find new material, and quickly. One of the pieces he remembered was the set of waltzes he had written for the Vienna Men's Chorus. He had not played it since, so no one in the Paris audience could have heard it before.

He wired home to Vienna and asked for the parts to be sent to him. Swiftly he orchestrated the piece, doing away with the voices, and performed it to a packed house.

Strauss retained the title of the poem that had been the

original inspiration for the piece, *'An der schönen blauen Donau'* ('By the Beautiful Blue Danube'). This time it received encore after encore. Word spread faster than a forest fire.

Back in Vienna the soft copper plates used by Strauss's publishing house wore out after producing 10,000 copies. Before the first print run was over, a hundred sets of plates had been worn out.

Johann Strauss had produced his most popular and enduring composition. He was now truly at the very pinnacle of his fame, the Strauss musical dynasty dominating music across Europe.

Things literally could not get better for the Waltz King. But they could get worse. The Strauss family enterprise was soon to endure its own *annus horribilis*.

Chapter 12

The Strauss Family in Mourning

Josef Strauss, meanwhile, was fast fulfilling his elder brother's opinion that he was the finer composer of the two. Works were pouring from this reluctant musician, and those in the know were of the opinion that the best of them were better than the works of his elder brother.

One was a waltz entitled *'Mein Lebenslauf ist Lieb' und Lust'* ('My Life is One of Love and Joy'), a delightful – even boisterous – waltz with octave leaps, but with passages of unexpected poignancy.

Delightful and boisterous it might have been but its title could not have been more inappropriate. Josef's health had never been good. He suffered from intermittent headaches, which became less intermittent and more and more intense as the years progressed. His habit of smoking up to twenty cigars a day did not help. Increasingly these headaches would lead to fainting fits.

An underlying ailment was undoubtedly exacerbated by increasing tension and rivalry between the three Strauss brothers. While Johann and Josef were away performing in Pavlovsk for the 1869 season, Eduard took advantage of their absence to assert his authority. He not only elevated himself to conductor of the Strauss Orchestra in Vienna, but announced plans to tour independently with it.

Word reached Pavlovsk and Josef was furious, even more so than his elder brother. The tension this caused spilled over. When Johann told Josef they needed a new polka and asked Josef to write it, he refused point-blank. In some despair Johann put pen to paper. Josef, no doubt somewhat stung with guilt, provided considerable assistance, and together they composed the much needed new polka. Ironically, it is one of the lightest, most memorable and best known of all Strauss polkas, '*Pizzicato-Polka*', which to this day bears the names of both brothers on the title page.

A measure of the tension between the three brothers, and the effect it was having, comes in an anguished letter written to them by Anna in the autumn of 1869:

> *[I] do not sleep, cannot eat, no rest, nothing but cunning, strife and* envy *among you – [I] will not tolerate any more, you are concerned with nothing but* your

own families, *and we are the whipping-boys … May*
God one day forgive you for it. I have not deserved
this ingratitude.

She clearly feared that if relations between the three brothers continued to deteriorate, the whole Strauss enterprise
would collapse – an enterprise she had done so much to
create and sustain.

But she would never know if her worst fears were to
materialise. On 23 February 1870, at the age of sixty-
eight, Anna died from 'suppuration of the lungs'. Her
sons were devastated, cancelling a raft of engagements.
Tensions were not helped by Johann yielding to an obsessive, almost irrational, fear of sickness and death, staying
away from the Hirschenhaus and refusing to attend his
mother's funeral.

Some months before, Josef had signed a contract to
conduct the following May in Warsaw. The terms had not
been favourable, committing Josef to a gruelling schedule,
but he had signed at a time when relations between the
brothers were at their worst, and when he was openly expressing a desire to be free and independent.

On 17 April, less than two months after his mother's
death, Josef gave a farewell concert in Vienna, then – tired
almost to the point of exhaustion – he left for Warsaw.
Things went wrong from the outset.

At the Polish border customs officials refused to allow musical instruments, as well as sheet music, through.

That was eventually solved, but on arrival in Warsaw the promised accommodation was unavailable. Far more important than these hitches was the fact that a number of musicians failed to arrive in Warsaw, due to a mix-up on the part of the musical agents.

Everything had to be delayed. Josef wired frantically to Eduard to send musicians from Vienna, at the same time scouring Warsaw for local talent. On 17 May, two days after the scheduled opening concert, Josef wrote to Johann:

> *I am disconsolate. No prospect of beginning. When this letter has reached your hands, the catastrophe will have reached its highest peak.*

Little did Josef know what an understatement that would be.

The first concert finally took place on 22 May, and was well received. Five days later Josef cancelled his subsequent appearance because he was unwell. He next stood in front of the orchestra on 1 June.

Things seemed to be going well until it came time to play Josef's latest composition, a medley entitled *'Musikalisches Feuilleton'* ('Musical Supplement').* In a particularly tricky passage, strings and wind began to pull apart.

Josef gestured frantically, trying to give the beat, but

---

* Unpublished and now lost.

the orchestral sections pulled further apart. With unerring inevitability, the piece was coming off the rails. Josef suddenly staggered, lost his footing, fell from the podium, and cracked his head as he tumbled to the floor.

Bleeding from the nose and ears, he was carried back to his apartment. His wife Karoline rushed to Warsaw, where she found Josef with 'his limbs paralysed, scarcely able to speak', as Eduard later wrote.

Johann, accompanied by Jetty, followed, but not until the end of the month. He himself was in poor health (again). This time he was suffering from jaundice. In the first week of July doctors in Warsaw were attending to both Johann and Josef Strauss.

Johann was well enough to lead the orchestra at three concerts later in that first week. Josef's condition, by contrast, had not improved. Karoline decided to move Josef back to Vienna, where medicine was more advanced and there would be no language problems.

The two-day carriage journey can only have exacerbated Josef's illness. On arrival in Vienna his condition was clearly critical. Doctors diagnosed a probable brain tumour, which would have accounted for the fainting spells, as well as the sudden loss of consciousness on the podium.

On the afternoon of 22 July 1870, one month short of his forty-third birthday, Josef died. Doctors asked permission of Karoline to carry out a post-mortem so they could establish if suspicions of a brain tumour were correct, but Karoline was adamant in her refusal. Accordingly the inquest found that Josef had died of 'decomposition of the blood', and the true cause of his tragically early death will never be known.

Josef was buried alongside his mother in the Strauss family grave in the St Marx Cemetery outside the city boundary of Vienna.* Once again, as with their mother, Johann Strauss did not attend the funeral.

The decade that began with trauma for Johann Strauss would have more shattering news for him before it was finished, but in the year following the double deaths in the family he was distracted by a visit from an Irish-born composer by the name of Patrick Sarsfield Gilmore.†

Gilmore had been put in charge of organising the World's Peace Jubilee and International Music Festival planned for the following summer in Boston. Everything about it was to be big. It would feature massive ensembles made up of several bands, and a huge coliseum was to be specially built, holding tens of thousands of people. Gilmore wanted, as his star turn, the Johann Strauss Or-

---

* Where, seventy-nine years earlier, Mozart had been buried in a common grave. The cemetery was closed to burials in 1874, but restored in the early twentieth century and opened to the public.

† Best known for writing the lyrics to the American Civil War song 'When Johnny Comes Marching Home'.

chestra with its founder at its head.* After Boston, Gilmore assured Strauss he would arrange dates in New York, to increase his popularity even more, as well as bringing in considerably increased fees.

If there was just one market left for Strauss to conquer, it was the United States, and what a market it could be. Huge audiences guaranteed, fees that in Europe Strauss could only dream of, and the final cementing of him as a *world*-renowned musician.

Which makes it all the more surprising that he had no desire to go. The reason gives us an insight into Strauss's character. In fact the whole trip – which he finally agreed to under pressure from Jetty, which lasted less than a month, and of which he hated every minute – gives us perhaps the most complete picture we have of Strauss as a man, thanks to the diligence of the American press.

I have already described Strauss's fear and detestation of anything to do with death. Well, he had a morbid fear of any activity that could lead to it too, and that included a sea voyage across the Atlantic. Accordingly, on 19 May 1872, two weeks before the planned departure, Strauss drew up his Last Will and Testament, naming his wife as his sole heir and main beneficiary.†

He expressed this fear of death, albeit in somewhat

---

* He also invited Giuseppe Verdi, who – busy preparing *Aida* for its world premiere in Cairo – turned him down.

† Maybe he realised his fear was unnecessary, since he knew perfectly well Jetty would be travelling with him.

laconic tones, to Gilmore himself as one of the reasons for his initial refusal to go. 'And what happens when your Indians massacre me?' he asked.*

Once in New York he addressed the possibility of a violent end in an interview with a reporter from the *Sun* newspaper: 'I want to mention something else to you that is perfectly awful, monstrous. There are no *Fahnwächter* [flagmen] on the railroads here. It is perfectly monstrous.'

Jetty, in the hotel room for the interview, confirmed Strauss's fear. 'My husband says he'd rather be killed swiftly, and be done with it, than to take another trip on an American railroad. He knows he'd be a dead man anyhow.'

The reporter for the *Sun* describes Strauss as 'tall, good-looking, with a black moustache, long flowing black whiskers, a fine forehead, black hair which is brushed back, a quick expressive eye, and an honest genial expression of countenance'.

Other accounts concur except in the matter of Strauss's height. The same newspaper, reviewing a concert, says he seems a 'quite handsome, dark-haired, pale-faced little man, with a gentlemanly bearing and genteel figure'. In the same review it sees 'something wild, goblin-like, almost maniacal, we might say, about the man when under the inspiration of music … who seemed surprised and pleased at the storm of applause which greeted him, causing him

---

* A fear not entirely without substance. Europe was awash with stories about encounters between settlers and Native Americans, and while Strauss was in America at least two massacres occurred.

to bow again and again, and a dozen times more before he could find the opportunity to begin'.

The German language *New-Yorker Staats-Zeitung* (New York State Newspaper) describes him as a 'small energetic man with curly black hair', and again as 'the little man in the black tails'.

The *New York Herald*, in colourful language, depicts a 'mercurial little man, who conducts with fiddle, bow, head, arms and legs, and even his coat tail seems instinct [*sic*] with expression'.

The *Sun* again writes of 'Strauss, the man-torpedo'. Its reporter, in the most comprehensive interview that Strauss gave, makes the point that he speaks no English, unlike his wife Jetty, who greeted the reporter 'cordially, and addressed him in very good English … She was dressed with exquisite taste after the latest Viennese fashion.'

With Jetty alongside him, Strauss sat opposite the *Sun* reporter (who was conversant in German) with, one imagines, a long face and sour mood, since he criticised almost every aspect of the country he was in.

Reporter How did you like Boston?

Herr Strauss I did not like it. Boston is Puritanical, stupid, dull. There is no life in the street. There is no display of elegance or luxury. The women are unattractive and do not dress nicely. I don't like Boston. But [possibly to humour his interviewer] with New York I am perfectly charmed.

Reporter When do you compose, in the daytime or at night?

Herr Strauss Always at night. I don't know of a single waltz that I composed in the daytime. *Der über Herrgott!* [Dear God Almighty!] Do you know how much I pay here for a shave? Fifty cents! Fifty cents! A whole *gulden*! *Ist das nicht schauderhaft?* [Isn't that appalling?] There is one thing that is very poor here, the beer. Ah! as far as that goes, this country is truly lacking.

Reporter I thought the beer here was better than in Germany.

Herr Strauss Oh! dear, dear, no! No comparison. It's dreadful here, and I am actually sick for want of our delightful Vienna beer.

Frau Strauss *(Chiming in, in support of her husband)* The beer is thick and heavy here. Oh! it's very poor.

Herr Strauss *(Smacking his lips and throwing himself back in his chair, in an attitude of rapture)* The beer in Vienna is divine, divine *[göttlich]*. Go to Vienna, drink beer, and die. *Göttlich, göttlich! [Then, probably realising he really did need to humour his interviewer]* But in every

The cover of *By the Beautiful Blue Danube*, Johann Strauss the Younger's most popular work.

Emperor Franz Josef I dancing the waltz at the annual Viennese Ball.

Johnann Strauss the Elder, founder of the most popular and prolific musical dynasty in history.

Joseph Lanner, close friend and later bitter rival of Johann Strauss the Elder.

Johann Strauss liked to compose standing at a desk. This hand-coloured lantern slide shows him on the verandah of his country house in Bad Ischl in 1880 (see pages 158 and 213).

Josef Strauss; his elder brother Johann considered him the more gifted musician.

Eduard Strauss, always stylish and immaculately turned out, never really got on with his elder brother Johann, and lost a fortune due to the profligacy of his wife and sons.

Elisabeth of Bavaria, known to history as Sisi, beautiful, rebellious, unstable, in the famous 1864 portrait by Franz Xaver Winterhalter. She was totally unsuited to the role of Empress of Austria, hated the formality of court life, and never adapted to it.

Universally respected by his people, and their emperor for sixty-eight years, Franz Josef witnessed his family devastated by untold tragedies.

This portrait by Franz von Lenbach, made in 1895 when Strauss was sixty-nine, captures the man more accurately than any photograph.

Strauss standing on the veranda of his villa with Johannes Brahms, two great composers who enjoyed each other's company. One is nearly eight years older than the other.

Johann Strauss statue in Vienna's Stadtpark, reputed to be the most photographed subject in Vienna, has formed the romantic image of Strauss the world knows, far removed from the difficult and obsessive character those close to him knew.

> other respect New York is charming.
> Life here must be very pleasant. New
> York is much more lively than London.
> What a bustle, what an uproar there is
> here all the time.

At that point in the interview Strauss was called away, and Jetty seized the moment for a little name-dropping. She told the reporter that her husband often went strolling in the Imperial Gardens at Schönbrunn Palace, opposite their house in Hietzing. He is always admitted, she said, and the emperor himself makes a point of always coming over and greeting him with a friendly, *'Grüss Sie Gott, wie gehts?'* ('God greet you, how are you?').

She made sure the reporter was aware her husband was a Knight of the Order of Franz Josef, and always received a standing ovation at court festivities. Jetty was more than just an efficient organiser, she was a brilliant PR woman as well.

This single interview, published in the *Sun of New York* on Saturday, 13 July 1872, I find utterly compelling. It tells us more about Johann Strauss the man than any number of musicological treatises on his compositions. What a beguiling image it conjures up of the most popular composer and orchestral leader *in the world* walking along the streets of New York in foul mood, wishing he had never come, disgusted at the price of getting a shave, with not even the satisfaction of a decent beer with which to cheer himself up!

He claimed to his interviewer that he was charmed by New York – though that is more likely to have been intended to flatter the journalist, particularly given his views on shaving and beer – and one wonders whether his opinions might have been improved a mere decade or so later, when the first skyscrapers went up, followed by the iconic Statue of Liberty.

Musically his performances were a triumph, but not to him. He was not particularly impressed that US President Ulysses S. Grant attended the afternoon concert at the Peace Jubilee in Boston on Tuesday 25 June (he was well used to playing before royalty and heads of state). And as for the performances he gave, don't believe a word of what he wrote to the *Neue Freie Presse* in Vienna, extolling 'my joyful experience in this extraordinary affair'.

The truth came in a letter he later wrote to a friend. He uses coruscating language, criticising every aspect of these gigantic performances, and using considerable exaggeration for effect. This is the same Strauss angry at the cost of a shave, disgusted at the taste of beer, wishing he had never made the journey to the United States. He obviously feels his initial instincts not to go were correct. Clearly nothing anybody could do – including Jetty – to cheer him up was successful. He must have been a difficult man to deal with in those few short weeks.

That letter, which so perfectly captures his stubbornness and irascibility, is worth quoting in full:

On the concert platform were thousands of singers and instrumentalists, and I had to conduct them! A hundred assistant conductors had been placed at my disposal to control these gigantic masses, but I was only able to see those nearest to me. Although we had rehearsed, an artistic performance, a proper production, was unthinkable. I would have put my life at risk if I had refused to appear … Suddenly a cannon fired, a gentle hint for us twenty thousand to begin the concert. 'The Beautiful Blue Danube' was on the programme. I gave the signal, my hundred sub-conductors followed me as quickly and as well as they could, and then a fearful racket broke out that I shall never forget as long as I live! As we had begun more or less together, my whole attention was now directed towards seeing that we should also finish together. Thank Heaven, I also managed that. The hundred thousand-strong audience roared their approval, and I breathed a sigh of relief when I found myself in the fresh air again and felt the firm ground beneath my feet. The next day I had to flee an army of impresarios, who promised me the whole of California for a tour of America. I had already had quite enough of the so-called music festival, and returned to Europe with the very greatest possible speed.

Curmudgeonly to the end!

Among the favourites Strauss performed in the US was, as he stated in that letter, *'By the Beautiful Blue Danube'*

('The Blue Danube Madness', as the *Sun* described it) as well as *'Artist's Life'*, *'1001 Nights'*, *'New Vienna'*, *'Pizzicato-Polka'*, and several specially written new compositions including a waltz that featured *'The Star-Spangled Banner'* in its coda.

The US sojourn was a triumph, and earned Johann Strauss a small fortune. His worldwide fame was assured. Yet he looked back on it for the rest of his life as a disaster, something he wished he had never done. Many times in later years he was invited back, with ever more enticing offers. But he meant what he said in that letter. He never returned.

Chapter 13

Strauss Turns His Hand to Operetta

There might well have been an underlying cause of Johann Strauss's intractability during the American sojourn, and indeed before it, and it was artistic. There was a musical problem. Strauss knew it. The impresarios of Vienna – theatre directors, even music publishers – knew it. Most importantly of all, the people of Vienna, the all-important concertgoers and music lovers, knew it.

Strauss was a master of the waltz. The Viennese loved to dance, but there was something they loved more. They loved to go to the theatre. It goes back to the old Viennese dictum that one eye cries, the other laughs. It exactly matches the universal symbol for theatre – a laughing face alongside a crying one. And what sort of theatre did they love most? Musical theatre. Not opera, but a new art form that was sweeping Europe. Operetta. Lighter than opera

141

and without its complexities, generally of shorter duration, with a wealth of hummable and instantly memorable tunes. An evening's musical entertainment unlikely to depict tragedy and certain to raise many a smile.

Blame, first and foremost, a German-born composer resident in Paris from the age of fourteen, a certain Jacques Offenbach. Six years older than Strauss, by the 1870s he had written more than eighty operettas. *Eighty!* Several of them had been performed at Vienna's theatres to enthusiastic audiences. Across the Channel meanwhile, the partnership of W. S. Gilbert and Arthur Sullivan was beginning to make a name for itself.

Vienna's impresarios knew that a good operetta could fill a theatre, and they wanted more. In particular they wanted homegrown pieces that would capture the essence of Viennese humour, with copious expressions and jokes in local Viennese dialect. A bonus would be that they would not need translating, thereby saving costs, and local talent would be likely to be less expensive than Offenbach, whose financial demands were notorious.

They turned, naturally, to Johann Strauss as early as 1862 or 1863. Strauss was quick to say no. He had just married Jetty and was fully tied up with engagements both in Vienna and Pavlovsk.

He was pleased to have adequate reason to decline. He knew, instinctively, that composing for the theatre was not for him. He had little sense of theatre and lacked an intuitive dramatic sense. Asked once by a publisher to write down his reminiscences, he replied, 'This has to do with words. For me words have always been difficult and demanding.'*

But he reckoned without the formidable Jetty. From the first time that her husband had been approached and asked to write an operetta, Jetty had encouraged him. Her motives were twofold. First, the practical incentive: works for the stage, unlike music for dancing, attracted royalties. Second, Jetty had been a professional singer. She knew the art form and she knew the people associated with it. She understood how to talk to theatre managers.

Jetty was the one person who knew how to influence Johann Strauss. There is a story that the manager of the Theater an der Wien – the small privately owned theatre outside the city centre which was a favourite of Beethoven's and had seen the premiere of many of his works, including the first version of his only opera *Fidelio*, but which now specialised in lighter musical theatre – entered into a charming conspiracy with Jetty.

He persuaded her to steal some of her husband's manuscripts. He then employed librettists to put words to the pieces. One morning a group of singers turned up at the Strausses' house in Hietzing, gathered round the piano, and sang Strauss's music to him, with words. Given that, as far as I am aware, none of these vocal versions

---

* Echoes of Beethoven who, asked why he did not write more opera, replied that when he heard music in his head, it was always the sound of the instruments of the orchestra, not the human voice.

has survived, the story is unlikely to be true. But its existence attests to the efforts that were being made to persuade Strauss to attempt operetta, and Jetty's leading role in the persuasion.

Whatever the tactics, Strauss respected his wife's business and artistic acumen, and some time in the early 1860s he began to compose operetta.

Word quickly spread about this new direction, but Strauss was not saying a word. He rebuffed all attempts to make him talk about it. He knew he needed to learn a new art form, and that it would be a struggle. He wanted to be left alone while he turned his hand to it.

He did not underestimate the challenge. Despite the Viennese newspapers announcing in January 1864 that Strauss would soon produce his first stage work, his first two attempts – *Don Quichotte* and *Romulus* – were stillborn. Strauss had actually completed two acts of *Romulus* before abandoning it. Things were not going well for him in the field of operetta.

Strauss was content to put operetta to one side while he concentrated on appearances in Pavlovsk and a full concert schedule at home. Then in October 1868 Jetty let the cat out of the bag by writing to a friend that Johann had declined offers to appear in Frankfurt, London and America, because he wanted to spend the winter 'working on an opera for the Wiedner Theatre'.*

---

* The old name for the Theater an der Wien.

The newspapers soon knew about it, and on 6 November 1868 *Die Presse* announced that Strauss was near to completing an operetta which he had entitled *Die lustigen Weiber von Wien* ('The Merry Wives of Vienna').

It appears never to have been performed, and is now lost. But Strauss had caught the bug, or more likely Jetty kept up an encouragement offensive, greatly helped by an amazing deal that was on offer. In return for signing an exclusive contract with the Theater an der Wien for the seasons 1870–1 and 1871–2, Strauss was offered a raft of benefits, of which the most attractive was a guaranteed 10 per cent share in the profits on the *gross* receipts of each performance.

There was no way Jetty was going to let him turn that down. And so he tried again, this time with the story of Ali Baba, which premiered to a full house on 10 February 1871 as *Indigo und die vierzig Räuber* ('Indigo and the Forty Thieves').

To say that reaction was mixed is an understatement. The highly respected music critic of *Neue Freie Presse*, Eduard Hanslick, was unremittingly scathing. He slated the 'dreadful libretto [which] provides the composer with no characters ... but with stuffed dolls which have neither point nor reason'. And in the event that Strauss was under any illusion that the criticism was aimed more at the librettists than at him, he had to suffer the indignity of reading this:

> *A man of Johann Strauss's reputation and talent*
> *would have done better not to have had anything to*
> *do with it … If only it had been over quickly. But*
> *this 'operetta' lasts almost four hours!*

The *Fremdenblatt* newspaper disagreed. It considered 'the whole thing an estimable piece of work' which promised 'the most splendid expectations for the future'.

In fact both were close to the mark, one in the short term, one in the long. *Indigo* actually played for forty-six performances at the Theater an der Wien, with further productions across Austria, Hungary and Germany, finally reaching Paris in 1875. But after that, it disappeared.*

It was soon after returning to Vienna from the Berlin premiere of *Indigo* that Strauss received the visit from Patrick Gilmore that led to the trip to the United States. For the moment, any question of another attempt at writing operetta was put aside.

But only for the moment. Max Steiner, co-director of the Theater an der Wien, was convinced Strauss had the potential to write a truly successful operetta, and in that

---

* Strauss, like many great composers, was not one to waste a good tune. Some passages from all his failed operettas resurfaced later in different forms and in other works.

belief he knew he could count on Jetty as an ally.*

He was right. The origin of the best operetta ever written is convoluted. All that matters to us is that some time around the middle of 1873 Strauss began to write a comic piece based on a fanciful plot involving a lawyer exacting revenge on his financier friend Eisenstein by taking him to a party, just before he is due to go to prison briefly for insulting an official, knowing his friend's wife will be there in disguise. There will, the lawyer knows, be flirting, infidelity and plenty of champagne drunk.

Die Fledermaus ('The Bat'), named for the costume the lawyer wore when *he* was the subject of an earlier practical joke at the hands of Eisenstein, was born. Legend has it that in a white heat of creativity Strauss sketched out much of the score in just '42 days and nights'. Certainly he worked quickly. The operetta was all but completed in two months.

Die Fledermaus premiered at the Theater an der Wien on Easter Sunday of the following year, with Strauss himself conducting. It got off to a stuttering start, but only because the theatre was already committed to staging performances of other works by a touring Italian company. Things were not helped later by the mezzo-soprano singing the role of Count Orlofsky becoming ill.†

---

* Steiner's grandson, also Max, was known as the 'father of film music'. He composed over 300 film scores, winning three Academy Awards, although not, inexplicably, for his best known, *Gone with the Wind*.

† From the first performance to this day, this male role is taken by a female singer.

In the autumn *Die Fledermaus* had the theatre to itself, and a new young actor and tenor in the role of the notary, Dr Falke. This was Alexander Girardi, who was to become the most famous operetta star in Vienna, forever associated with the music of Johann Strauss.

The production was a triumph. A month later, in July 1874, it opened in Berlin and spread swiftly to theatres across Germany. Soon it would be staged across Europe, before crossing the Atlantic to America, and much further afield to Australia. In December 1876 it became the first Strauss operetta to be performed in London, and the following year it reached Paris.*

A number of years later, in 1894, *Die Fledermaus* was to receive its highest musical compliment. That *über*-serious, deeply emotional composer Gustav Mahler, in his capacity as music director of the staid, conservative, traditional Vienna Court Opera, introduced the 'operetta of all operettas' into the repertoire.

It played to packed houses, but there is a suggestion that even an admirer such as Mahler felt it a shame that Viennese audiences seemed to favour operetta over more heavyweight opera. This was, after all, the city of Mozart, Beethoven, Schubert, Brahms – and, albeit briefly, Wagner.

After a sell-out on a hot August day, Mahler said to a colleague:

---

* Substantially revised and under a new title, *La Tzigane* ('The Gypsy Girl').

Excellent [that it's a sell-out], but it's Fledermaus *instead of* Walküre, *which I gave the night before last. I value* Fledermaus *and am pleased that it brings in money, but it is nonetheless sad that* Fledermaus *packs the house, and not* Walküre.

So what is it about *Die Fledermaus*, which seemed to come out of nowhere after a string of failed attempts, even flops, from Strauss that makes it the best-loved, most enduring of all Viennese operetta, to the extent that the *still* conservative and traditional Vienna State Opera stages a new production every New Year's Eve?

It is, of course, light-hearted, even superficial, with an utterly implausible plot. But then what operetta does not fit that description? Above all, it is *fun*. I have been known to sit through an entire production with a smile from ear to ear that never fades. Its centrepiece is a boisterous party, a ball. The first act leads up to it, and the third act unravels the knotty relationships that are formed at the event.[*]

The main characters may seem one-dimensional at first, but there is more to them than meets the eye. Eisenstein is happy to deceive his wife, but then falls completely in love with her when she is in disguise at the

---

[*] Modern directors delight in putting star turns into Count Orlofsky's ball, characters who otherwise take no part in the performance. In 1990 the great Australian soprano Dame Joan Sutherland was joined on stage at Covent Garden by tenor Luciano Pavarotti and mezzo-soprano Marilyn Horne for several numbers to mark her retirement.

ball. His wife Rosalinde is just as happy to deceive him, but is determined to capture him because she actually loves him deeply. The maid Adele, from the lower classes, might appear vulgar to her employers, but just marvel at the class she shows at the ball when she tries to convince Eisenstein she is a proper lady!*

Over and above every other consideration there is the music. Strauss never wrote a better overture. It sparkles from first note to last. There is gaiety in every note. In the operetta itself there are so many instantly memorable melodies that you leave the theatre with them tumbling around in your head, jostling for priority.

There is, however, one other consideration, one further factor, that contributed to its success in Vienna, and it has nothing to do with Strauss.

Eleven months before *Die Fledermaus* opened, Vienna decided anything London and Paris could do, it could do better, and on 1 May 1873 it opened a World Exhibition. It was a project of gigantic proportions designed to show off the best of everything Vienna had to offer in the fields of technology and medicine, fashion and interior design. It took the form of a vast display in the Prater public park and VIPs from across the developed world were invited.

The timing of the show could not have been worse. A cholera epidemic was sweeping the city, which put guests

---

* Her aria *'Mein Herr Marquis'* is, I think, one of the most seductive and beguiling in all operetta, or opera for that matter, on a par with Musetta's waltz, *'Quando me'n vo'* in Act II of *La Bohème*.

off and prevented the public from flocking to attend. Then, on 9 May, there came the great crash of the Vienna Stock Exchange. This was Black Friday. In a classic foretaste of crashes to come in succeeding centuries, too many shares had been issued for too many unsound enterprises. Too many credit notes had been issued, too much money lent. When it all came crashing down, fortunes were lost overnight, resulting in bankruptcy and suicide among Vienna's moneyed class.

In the ensuing months the number of visitors to the World Exhibition picked up, but the project was doomed. Vienna's World Exhibition closed at the end of the year with a huge and crippling deficit of almost 15 million gulden.

A mere four months later *Die Fledermaus* opened, and what was its central message? That happy is he who is able to forget what he cannot change.* In other words, whatever happened wasn't your fault. It was beyond your control. No need for you to be concerned about it.

So whose fault was it? And what is the remedy? The famous song right at the end of the operetta spells it out. It was all the fault of champagne – that king of wines – and champagne can make it all better again. 'So let us drink a toast to King Champagne the First!'†

It was *precisely* the message the bruised and battered Viennese wanted to hear, and it is precisely the message any

---

* See chapter 1, page 6.

† 'Jubelnd wird Champagner/Der Erste sie genannt!'

person from that day to this, buffeted by ill fortune, wants to hear: the pop of a cork, and the effervescence of bubbles poured into a glass.

The central message of *Die Fledermaus* might be pretty basic, and it might not bear too close an examination. But it speaks to all people of all generations. There are few people who do not appreciate being told to open a bottle and enjoy themselves.

Johann Strauss and his superb librettists Karl Haffner and Richard Genée had created an operetta that would endure for all time.

Strauss was not finished with the operetta form. In the ensuing twenty-three years he would produce no fewer than thirteen more operettas. Only two – *Eine Nacht in Venedig* ('One Night in Venice') and *Der Zigeunerbaron* ('The Gypsy Baron') – achieved any sort of lasting success, and both pale before the supreme example of *Die Fledermaus*.

Four years and two forgettable operettas after *Die Fledermaus*, Strauss was working on a new project. It was an operetta entitled *Blinde Kuh* ('Blind Man's Buff'). His newfound enthusiasm for operetta – fuelled by the success of *Die Fledermaus* – was undimmed, and Jetty was unstinting in her encouragement.

While Strauss was in Paris conducting at the new Paris Opéra, clearly longing to return to Jetty and their home in Hietzing, Jetty wrote to a friend on 20 October 1877, 'Jean is being drawn to Hietzing by his work desk – where, waiting longingly for him, is "Blinde Kuh".'

But Jetty was never to see this new operetta. On 8 April 1878 she suffered a heart attack and at 11.30 p.m. she died.

Chapter 14

Johann Strauss Tastes Failure

In eight short years Johann Strauss had lost his mother, his brother and his wife. His reaction each time seemed to surpass what was normal. Grief is one thing, but Strauss's behaviour bordered on the irrational. His morbid fear of anything to do with death led him to stay away from the funerals of his mother and brother, as I have recounted. Now, once again, his reaction was extreme.

He not only refused to attend Jetty's funeral, he adamantly refused to have anything to do with arranging it. As with the previous two deaths in the family, his younger brother Eduard was left to make all the arrangements. This was such a clear abrogation of duty that it caused considerable antagonism on Eduard's part.

Johann went further. The same night he found Jetty's lifeless body, he fled the house in Hietzing that was their home and never set foot inside it again. He took refuge in Eduard's house and told him he wanted nothing to do with what now needed to be done. Eduard was left to pick up the pieces. It was Eduard who had the body taken away, Eduard who arranged the funeral, walked behind the coffin, and dealt with the legal formalities.

Johann, we know, had a horror of death and everything associated with it, but in this case it might have been exacerbated by the unquestionable fact that his marriage had been running into trouble. The seven-year age gap began to show as Strauss turned fifty years of age, and Jetty drew closer to sixty. Her health had not been good for some time. She was prone to speak of herself as 'a poor old cripple', and infirmity had robbed her of her looks, and to a certain extent her charm. Her ill health cannot have helped marital relations and might even have contributed to their deterioration.

There was also the issue of her complicated former life. It is possible Strauss was aware only of the two illegitimate daughters Jetty had by Baron Todesco, and not of the five others. Certainly he was taken totally by surprise when, in the autumn of 1876, a young man turned up at the Hietzing house, addressed Jetty as 'mother', and asked for money.

Strauss threw him out of the house, but the man then wrote to his mother asking for money, making increasingly unreasonable demands. On the day of her death she received a letter from her son that apparently amounted to blackmail. Strauss had no hesitation in saying it was the shock of this letter that induced the fatal heart attack.

It had been an open secret in Viennese musical circles for some time that the Strausses' marriage had become rocky, and Strauss was known to have developed a roving eye. It had roved particularly towards a young actress by the name of Angelika Dittrich, who had come to Vienna in search of a theatrical career.

Strauss first met her in the lobby of the Hotel Victoria, where he had taken up residence after leaving the house in Hietzing. He was immediately attracted to the pretty, vivacious young woman, who lost no time in telling him she had loved his music since childhood, flattering him with almost every word she uttered.

Angelika, known as Lili, was intelligent enough to know that looks alone were not enough for her to make her name as an actress, and that she had more looks than talent. Her ambition therefore was to enter theatre management, and she knew there was no one in Vienna who could be of more use to her than the famous Johann Strauss.

As for Strauss, the unremitting attention of a pretty young woman was irresistible. He apparently did not consider the age difference of twenty-five years to be any sort of barrier, and after a whirlwind romance Strauss and Lili were married. It was just seven weeks since Jetty had died.

Strauss's choice of bride this time was as unfortunate as his first choice had been serendipitous. Lili did not realise what she had taken on. Johann Strauss was what we would today call a workaholic. When the creative spark was in him he simply could not stop, and it was in him for much of the time.

We have already seen Strauss himself tell the *New York Sun* reporter that he always composed at night. Another journalist, a German this time, gives a riveting account of Strauss's compulsive work ethic, and his extraordinary, and frankly inexplicable, lack of self-confidence. He also describes how utterly essential Jetty was to her husband's creative process:

> *Strauss works 'feverishly'. He composes with the same nervous energy with which he conducts the orchestra. His workroom is everywhere. In a velvet suit and top boots, his hair in a mess, he rushes through his apartments ... Madame Strauss sees to it that in every room there is a table with writing implements ... Whether Strauss is composing an operetta or a polka, he gets into an indescribable state of nervous excitement. After two or three hours of such work, he is as exhausted as a native bearer ... Strauss always believes that his best work is already behind him. He belongs to that breed of artists who spend their lives doubting themselves.*

There is a photograph of Strauss, some years later, showing him at his composing desk – standing up!* This is how he preferred to compose, and it perfectly fits the journalist's description of him as composing in a fit of nervous energy.

Later still, a portrait by the celebrated German painter Franz von Lenbach captures to perfection the tortured, almost manic, intensity of Johann Strauss. His eyes are blazing and his jaw is set, as if he is imploring the artist to be done so he can get back to work.†

This was decidedly not the kind of man Lili thought she was taking on. She had anticipated a glamorous life in theatrical circles, attending premieres, soirées, attracting admiring glances as she walked on the arm of the famous Johann Strauss, a man universally admired but belonging to her.

To an extent this happened, at least in the early months of their marriage – Strauss as keen to show off his beautiful young wife as she was ready to play the part. But no one with Strauss's ferocious appetite for work could behave like that for long.

Some years earlier, with money earned from the eventual success of *Die Fledermaus*, Jetty had persuaded Strauss to purchase two adjacent plots of land in the Wieden district

---

* See plate section, page 3.

† I believe that in this painting Lenbach gives us a more insightful portrait of Strauss than any photograph.

of Vienna. She knew that, much as he hated the social whirl that accompanied the musical life, he needed to play the role and play it in a manner befitting his status. The villa in Hietzing was neither impressive enough, nor close enough to the city centre, to enable him to do this.

The land bought, Jetty supervised the construction of a luxury mansion – a *Stadt-Palais* ('city palace') – that would meet his every need. Apparently (despite the German journalist's depiction of Strauss as all work and no play) he did have a passion for billiards. Jetty ensured the new house had a billiard room, as well as stables, and a large and elegant reception room where he could entertain eminent guests.

Jetty did not live to see the building completed. After their honeymoon in Wyk, with its beautiful if rather windswept beaches, on the North Frisian Island of Föhr in the North Sea, Strauss and his new wife moved into the newly completed mansion on the Igelgasse in an exclusive district of Vienna.*

The reception room was everything Jetty had wanted it to be, and here Strauss entertained such eminent musical guests as Johannes Brahms, Anton Bruckner and Giacomo Puccini. A contemporary print shows Strauss seated at a large ornate desk, dressed in a sharply cut and immaculately tailored suit, a bearskin rug under his feet, and a tasteful nude painting on the wall.

---

* Today the Johann-Strauss-Gasse.

These names and this lifestyle were totally unfamiliar to Lili. She was out of her depth and out of her class, and that twenty-five-year age gap must have weighed on her heavily. Matters were not helped – in fact they were considerably exacerbated – when Strauss's newly completed and much awaited new operetta, *Blinde Kuh*, premiered on 18 December 1878, less than seven months after Strauss and Lili were married.

Lili no doubt enjoyed a glittering evening at the Theater an der Wien, where all the talk was of the brilliant and charismatic Alexander Girardi in the principal role. The combination of Strauss and Girardi. What could possibly go wrong?

Everything. In fact there had been an ominous piece of bad luck in the run-up to the premiere. Several numbers Strauss had already composed were lost in the move to the new mansion. He was forced to compose twelve new numbers. Is it too fanciful to imagine him furiously accusing Lili of mislaying them, of not looking after his precious manuscripts properly, as Jetty surely would have done?

The operetta was a huge flop, in fact the only complete failure of his career, humiliatingly withdrawn after only sixteen performances. He could take small comfort that the inane libretto by one Rudolf Kneisel took most of the blame. Reviews were excoriating – 'Among his other talents, Johann Strauss also possesses that of selecting the worst possible text', and (the pun working in English as well as German), 'Johann Strauss personally conducts – the audience to the outside of the theatre.'*

Strauss had a secure enough reputation to survive a flop, particularly when it was the librettist who took most of the criticism. But it was another nail in the already fragile coffin that was his marriage to Lili.

His next operetta, the seventh, *Das Spitzentuch der Königin* ('The Queen's Lace Handkerchief'), received an opening-night ovation greater than any since *Die Fledermaus*, but fickle as these things are, it swiftly disappeared into obscurity, possibly sped on its way by the fact that at least four librettists, and subsequently even more, claimed a share of the profits, resulting in a messy court case.†

A similar fate befell the eighth, *Der lustige Krieg* ('The Merry War'), praised in the *Neue Freie Presse* as 'the work of a brilliant talent', but on this occasion the cause might have been something entirely unrelated, which devastated the city and changed Viennese theatrical life.

Less than two weeks after the opening of *Der lustige Krieg*, on 7 December 1881, the Ringtheater, one of the most imposing buildings on the still newly completed

---

* As always Strauss knew better than to waste a good tune. He reused several pieces from *Blinde Kuh*, most successfully the waltz *'Kennst du mich?'*, which was played by salon orchestras for decades afterwards.

† Strauss once again used the best material from it, fashioning it into one of his most popular waltzes, *'Rosen aus dem Süden'* ('Roses from the South').

Ringstrasse, presented the German-language premiere of Offenbach's hugely popular *Hoffmanns Erzählungen* ('The Tales of Hoffmann').

The following night, brilliant reviews combined with a public holiday ensured a full house. Minutes before the curtain rose, an ignition fault with the gas lighting backstage started a fire. It quickly spread unchecked across the auditorium, engulfing the audience. In total 386 people died in a tragedy unprecedented of its kind in the city's history.

In the long term it led to a complete overhaul of safety in theatres, with new and stricter regulations. In the short term people simply stayed away. A measure of Strauss's popularity is that *Der lustige Krieg*, playing at the Theater an der Wien, seemed to buck the trend, running for more than a hundred consecutive performances before it faded into relative obscurity.

In the previous year Strauss had purchased an imposing country retreat at Schönau-bei-Leobersdorf about twenty miles south-west of Vienna, to give him peace and quiet and an escape from the city and even from the house in Igelgasse, where he was constantly called on by visitors.

Musically speaking it was an inspired move; on a personal level a disaster. Strauss composed his two most popular operettas after *Die Fledermaus* at Schönau – *Eine Nacht in Venedig* ('One Night in Venice') and *Der Zigeunerbaron* ('The Gypsy Baron') – but it took him away from the city, the social whirl and the bright lights. Good for Strauss, not so good for his wife.

Lili still harboured ambitions to pursue a career in theatrical management. In May 1880 the director of the Theater an der Wien, Maximilian Steiner, died and his son Franz took over.

Lili knew father and son well from their dealings with Strauss – in fact Max Steiner is often credited for the making of Strauss as a composer of operetta. Whereas Steiner senior was a serious and dedicated theatre manager, whose premature death was said to have been brought on by the precarious finances of the theatre, his son was in another mould. A sole photograph shows an unsmiling young man, but with tousled dark hair and fashionable pencil moustache, and a bow tie tied at a louche angle. It is easy to imagine the face breaking into spontaneous laughter.

It is not exactly clear when Lili began an affair with Franz, but it was certainly under way in 1882, two years after the purchase of the villa in Schönau, when Lili was thirty-two years of age and Steiner three years younger.

It appears Strauss knew what was going on and did his best to win his wife back. On 28 July he wrote an imploring letter to her while she was in Franzensbad – whether with Steiner we do not know. The tone is not that of a world-famous musician at the height of his career and creative powers, more that of a lovelorn cuckold: 'Let yourself be well and truly kissed, dear Lili, but do not run away from me! Please stay!'

The language suggests he was even prepared to allow the affair to continue, as long as Lili stayed with him. She did not. She moved first into the Theater an der Wien with Steiner, achieving her ambition of helping him to run the theatre, then followed him to Berlin, where she leaves our story.*

Despite that letter, it transpires that Strauss himself might not only have been aware of his wife's infidelity but – as in his first marriage – might not have been entirely faithful himself.

In early November 1882, just four months after imploring Lili to stay with him, Strauss left Berlin, where he had been conducting *Der lustige Krieg*, for Pest to conduct the same operetta there. He did not travel alone. Accompanying him was a widow aged twenty-six – thirty-one years his junior – by the name of Adèle Strauss.

---

* In Berlin Lili and Steiner separated, and she ran her own photographic studio, 'Atelier Lili'. She later returned to Austria (though not Vienna), where she opened another studio. During the First World War she fostered two daughters abandoned by their mother and whose father had been sent to the Front. Lili often said she wished she had not left Strauss. Her foster daughters were fond of her, erecting a gravestone on her death in 1919, which read, 'Your goodness is not forgotten.'

Chapter 15

To the Altar Again

Johann Strauss had known Adèle for the best part of eight years, for the simple reason that after she married one Anton Strauss (no relation to the musical Strausses, the name was a complete coincidence) she moved into the rooms he occupied in the Hirschenhaus, the same capacious house into which Johann Strauss the elder had moved his growing family many decades before. The Strauss family had long since moved out, but Anton's father had acted as financial adviser to them, and it is likely there would have been meetings, or at least social gatherings, at the Hirschenhaus.

What is certain is that Johann Strauss and Adèle knew each other, and Adèle had frequently let Johann know she admired both him and his music. It was therefore natural, when Anton died suddenly after less than three years of marriage, leaving Adèle with a two-year-old daughter, that she would turn to Johann Strauss for comfort and advice.

A mutual attraction developed, and swiftly turned into something more. Johann declared his love for Adèle, deciding he wanted to spend the rest of his life with her, and she was eager to reciprocate.

It is worth pausing for a moment to look at how unlikely a match this was. Johann Strauss, now aged fifty-seven, married twice before, no children, world-famous composer and orchestral leader, and Adèle, aged twenty-six, widowed with a small child.

A cynic might say they each had plenty to gain, with an obvious affection for each other but no question of love. After all, they could be father and daughter. It is true there was mutual benefit. For Johann there was once again companionship, with the hope that – if the gods were smiling – Adèle might be able to organise his diary, keep house so he could devote himself to his music, generally look after him.

For Adèle, well, it would have been hard to resist Johann's gesture of love – an irrevocable annuity for life of 4000 gulden (roughly equivalent to £11,000 today). Also she must have known that a widow with a small child would be unlikely to attract an admiring young suitor. In these circumstances, when a comfortable and secure life beckoned, the enormous age difference was nothing more than a minor issue for her.

All true, but let us wind fast forward many years and see what actually happened. In the first place Johann and Adèle stayed together until Johann died seventeen years later in her arms. In the interim she more than filled the void left by Jetty, providing him with perfect conditions in which to work. In fact progress on *Eine Nacht in Venedig*, which had stalled due to domestic tensions with Lili, resumed and Strauss swiftly brought it to completion. The autograph score shows that Adèle herself copied out parts of the song texts. She was the perfect successor to Jetty, and more.

Johann's transformation, once Adèle moved into the house on the Igelgasse, was noticed by everyone. Friends commented that he had shed years, with the energy of a man half his age. It was now he began to dye his hair and moustache black, augmenting the youthful look. It was even rumoured he took to riding his horses at Schönau, which toned him up physically.

If anyone doubted Johann was in love, we have written proof. Almost daily he wrote her little love notes. On one occasion before going to the theatre to conduct, he left her a note saying, 'My dear Adèle! I shall change the tempo from *maestoso* to *allegro* so I can hurry back to you all the sooner and kiss you a few minutes earlier. Your Jean.' On another occasion: 'You are the queen of my happiness, of my life!' And again, when he was away in Berlin: 'Cherchez la femme. Sleep well, you black-eyed Adèle, the only woman on earth.' In what is quite possibly a rare acknowledgement of his age, one note read, 'Let us be merry, Adèle, on ne vit qu'une fois.'

If any doubters still needed persuading that Adèle was the perfect soulmate for Johann, it was provided in the unlikeliest of places, the pages of the normally scathing and satirical publication, *Der Floh* ('The Flea'), which waxed positively lyrical:

> *Maestro Johann Strauss … needs a comfortable, gracious home, if he is to create with a joyful heart, if the refreshing spring of his lovely melodies is to flow unrestricted. Frau Adèle Strauss will offer him such a home. She will have a beneficial effect upon his nervous artistic temperament, and will be happy if she can give again to the honoured and beloved composer the peace of mind and happiness necessary for his creativity.*

This paean is all the remarkable, even prescient, for the fact that it was published on 25 March 1883. Given that Johann's divorce from Lili was granted on 9 December 1882, before which it would have been unthinkable for Adèle to move in with him, it must have been written at the most three months after the relationship became public. The effect of having Adèle living with him really *did* transform Johann Strauss.

But there was a problem, a huge problem. Johann and Adèle could not marry, as long as Lili lived. The divorce might have been granted by the civil authorities, but it was not accepted by the Roman Catholic Church in Austria to which Johann belonged. In fact Johann applied for papal consent to the divorce immediately after it was granted, but the Vatican refused.

There was another obstacle too. Adèle was Jewish. Under Austrian law, a Roman Catholic was forbidden to marry a Jew.*

In each case there was a solution, but it was drastic. Adèle did not hesitate: she gave up her Jewish faith and converted to Protestantism. As for Johann, well, then as now, there is no religious law that cannot be bent with a little incentive mixed with a dose of hypocrisy.

Twenty years previously Johann had dedicated a polka *'Neues Leben'* ('New Life') to a member of the German aristocracy, Duke Ernst II of Saxe-Coburg, himself an excellent musician and amateur composer, perhaps better remembered as the elder brother of Queen Victoria's consort, Prince Albert.

The duke, an admirer of Johann Strauss, was suitably flattered and awarded him a decoration. If there was any debt still due to Strauss, this was the moment he called it in. On 8 December 1885 Johann Strauss formally renounced his Austrian citizenship. Five months later he applied to the City Magistrate of Coburg to become a citizen of Coburg, pledging a donation to the local fund for the poor to oil the bureaucratic wheels.

---

* The irony of this was that Strauss himself had Jewish blood, as we shall see later.

On 24 June 1886 his new citizenship was confirmed, and two weeks later he officially left the Roman Catholic Church and became a Lutheran Protestant. In July the following year Duke Ernst used the powers invested in him to dissolve Strauss's marriage to Lili, and five weeks after that Johann and Adèle were married at the Coburg Register Office, with a religious service later that day in the ducal church.

The whole procedure had taken an inconveniently long time to come to fruition – almost two years from the time Johann first applied to relinquish his Austrian citizenship to the day he married Adèle – but come to fruition it had.

Johann Strauss was now married for the third time. And Johann Strauss, born in Vienna, whose music distilled the very essence of Vienna and the Viennese into musical notes, whose compositions were named for the Vienna woods, the Blue Danube, Viennese blood, even the city of Vienna itself, was now a German citizen!

Johann Strauss had once again found happiness at home, but there was another area of his family life where relations were less pleasant, and this concerned his younger brother Eduard.

'Der schöne Edi' had not had an easy time of it. Rather like brother Josef he had not initially wanted a musical career, preferring to study for the diplomatic service. But again, as with Josef, his mother stepped in, decreeing that it was essential Eduard study music and enter the family firm. As I have already stated, she must have been overjoyed to find he did indeed possess musical talent. Once she knew that, there was no choice for Eduard but to join his brothers. He studied musical theory, as well as piano and violin. But here Johann intervened and pointed out that while there was no shortage of pianists and violinists, what was really needed was a harpist – they were much thinner on the ground. Johann, as well as being an established musician, was ten years older than Eduard, who therefore looked up to his brother in every respect.

Eduard studied the harp, but again like both his brothers he was soon composing as well as playing. In what can only be described as a quite extraordinary, I am sure unique, occurrence in any field of the arts, Eduard composed literally hundreds of pieces in his lifetime, as did Johann, Josef and indeed their father. Combine their compositions – and I am referring to works with opus numbers, in other words published music, as opposed to sketches – and it runs into the best part of 2,000. Not even the Bach family can rival that.

If Johann was king of the waltz, and Josef a waltz master too, Eduard specialised in the quick polka. Of all his compositions, it is polkas such as *'Bahn frei!'* ('Clear the track!'), *'Mit Dampf'* ('Steam up'), *'Ausser Rand und Band'* ('Out of control'), *'Ohne Bremse'* ('Brakes off'), which have remained in the repertoire – the novelty and excitement of rail travel clearly exercising a great influence on him.

Eduard, as we have seen, was soon playing harp in his brother's orchestra, but it was as a conductor that Eduard Strauss truly made his name. Of his debut as conductor in 1862, at the age of twenty-seven, the Viennese periodical *Der Zwischenakt* commented:

> *Herr Strauss was enthusiastically greeted, and presented with rare feeling and accuracy all the waltzes composed by his brother Johann during this season. His conducting showed that in him we have a conductor of the same calibre. Long live the Strauss trinity!*

One can imagine the mixed emotions this must have caused in Eduard. On the one hand praise for his conducting abilities, but always in the shadow of his eldest brother.

By all accounts Eduard was something of a tyrant on the podium. He would accept nothing but the very best from his musicians, and he was not afraid to show who was in charge. When, in the spring of 1878, forty-one members of the orchestra refused to undertake a six-month tour of Germany and Sweden, Eduard unhesitatingly dismissed them.

He had a harsh tongue too. On receiving what he called a 'perfectly impudent' letter from the orchestra's principal cellist asking for a pay rise, he unleashed a four-page torrent of abuse, blatantly impugning the unfortunate cellist's musical talents: '… you dare to ask me for a salary increase? Must I remind you that there are twenty-three cello pieces here that *you are unable* to play?'

And one can imagine the tones in which he was accustomed to address his players, judging by a comment he made about the wind section in a letter to a friend: 'This instrument [the 'Flutophone'] is *supposed* to replace two flutes … Oh my dear honoured friend! Would that you could find an instrument that would replace *all wind players* …'

You have to conclude that Eduard Strauss, excellent conductor though he might have been, was not well liked by his musicians, and was certainly nowhere near as loved as his eldest brother.

What made matters worse for the players was that it was Eduard, not either of his brothers, who most often conducted them. Johann was averse to touring. When he did so, it was under protest. Josef had always resented standing in for his eldest brother and, following his untimely death, touring duties fell to the youngest, Eduard, who was equally resentful.

You can see why. Such was the universal popularity of the Johann Strauss Orchestra, it was in demand literally across the world. Eduard himself estimated later in life that in twenty-three years of touring with the Strauss Orchestra he visited 840 towns in two continents and gave concerts at 14 Exhibitions.

And therein lay the problem for Eduard. It was the *Strauss* Orchestra, and that meant only one thing for audiences. Even before Josef's death, although it was acknowledged in Vienna that there were three Strauss brothers, it was always a case of Johann – the eldest – and the other two. After Josef's death, Johann's pre-eminence was all the more assured.

Eduard had one eye on posterity, and there was only one way to ensure that as a musician: as composer not conductor. Here Johann's name was assured in perpetuity, such was the brilliance of his compositions, and Eduard was a good enough musician to know that as composer he simply was not in his elder brother's class.

We know of at least 300 published pieces by Eduard, but it would appear there could have been many more. Difficult though it might be to believe for a Strauss, Eduard was not always able to get his work published. Johann remarked in 1892: '[Edi's] compositions are not bad – but nobody wants to buy them.'

As a conductor, though, he was feted wherever he took the orchestra, nowhere more so and at a higher social level than in Britain. He played before Queen Victoria at both Windsor Castle and Buckingham Palace, as his father had done before him.

The queen, exhibiting either a formidable memory or an efficient briefing by her advisers, said to Eduard, 'You remind me very much of your father. It seems like only yesterday that he played at my Coronation Ball.' In fact it was fifty-six years earlier.

After a concert at Windsor Castle the queen presented him with a silver writing set, in the hope that he would use the pen in writing his next composition. In mentioning composition rather than conducting she will have pushed completely the right button. She certainly knew how to flatter him!

Eduard was himself equally adept at flattery. In his letter of thanks he described the evening at Windsor Castle as 'one of the most beautiful and memorable of my artistic career', adding, 'I and my family will always remember Her Majesty and the Royal Family with undying veneration.'

Johann was well aware that, because of his nightly appearances on the rostrum at Vienna's leading dance halls, Eduard was considerably better known in person than he was himself. Edi was frequently pictured and caricatured in the newspapers, with reviews describing his performances in detail. The epithet 'der schöne Edi' had well and truly stuck.

Despite the fact that Johann had, in effect, engineered this situation by avoiding performing, it appears his brother's popularity did occasionally get to him. There is anecdotal evidence that he would introduce himself by saying, 'I am Edi's brother.'

At times the tension between eldest and youngest brothers simmered over, and it seems it was usually Johann, playing the role of *paterfamilias*, who resorted to corrective action. In 1892, after what must have been close to a bust-up between them (we do not know the circumstances), Johann felt obliged to write to his brother:

You still see everything pessimistically – you always think that I am trying to score points over you. For

*goodness' sake, why won't you rid yourself of such fool-
ish notions? How old do you have to become before you
finally realise that your brother is not your enemy? …
Sometimes our relationship has been worsened because
of your sheer ambition, but you should know that my
brotherly feelings towards you have never changed.*

'*How old do you have to become … ?*' This admonishing note
was written when Eduard was fifty-seven years of age!

Just how far relations between the two had deteriorated
would become clear when Johann's will, written in 1895,
omitted his brother entirely, on the grounds that 'he finds
himself in favourable circumstances'.

It is true that Eduard earned a considerable amount
of money as conductor of the Strauss Orchestra, not to
mention a wide assortment of medals, decorations, medals
of honour, golden snuffboxes, all the gifts a successful conductor can expect to have bestowed on him.

But Johann was not prepared to make changes to his
will when, two years later, Eduard's financial position suddenly changed, and much for the worse. A codicil stated
bluntly and unforgivingly:

*Although the reasons for which I did not remember
my dear brother Eduard in my will to my knowledge
no longer apply, I will not make any alteration to take
account of this. I hope that my brother's situation will
improve.*

So what accounted for Eduard's sudden reversal of fortune? Almost thirty-five years earlier, on 8 January 1863, Eduard had married Maria Magdalena Klenkhart, the youngest daughter of a coffee house owner who had been a friend of Johann Strauss the elder.

The couple had two sons, interestingly named Johann and Josef (one suspects Anna's controlling hand in this). We owe a debt of gratitude to Johann for carrying the Strauss musical tradition into the next century. But the two sons, in connivance with their mother, would later spend every penny of their father's hard-earned fortune, leaving him destitute.

As for Eduard himself, he would one day take revenge on his two brothers, after their deaths, in a devastating way, the consequences of which we are still suffering today.

Chapter 16

Tragedy in the Imperial Royal Family

The year is 1888 and Franz Josef has been Emperor of Austria for forty years. He is fifty-eight years of age, and already to his people he is 'the old emperor'. He has a kindly, avuncular face, a half-smile always present, eyes slightly closed, causing friendly wrinkles to emanate from their corners. He is universally respected, even if 'loved' is a touch too strong a word for a man who rules through divine providence.

Those who had predicted he would soon relinquish the throne after being placed there in fraught circumstances in 1848 had been long since proved mistaken. In fact he had won the affection and admiration of his people on that day in February 1853 when he had survived an assassination attempt. Where had he been at the time, and what had he been doing? Was he fulfilling some official function, surrounded by advisers and soldiers? No, he had been strolling with one of his officers, a good friend, on the Bastei, mingling easily with other Viennese following the same pursuit.

The high, sturdy collar of his military uniform had saved his life. What no one could have known at the time is that what, if the assassination attempt had succeeded, would have been a brief five-year reign, forgotten to history, was to become a reign lasting sixty-eight years, almost the longest to this day in European history.

But as the Viennese prepared to put on a show for Franz Josef's fortieth jubilee celebrations, neither for them nor their emperor had it been four decades of trouble-free existence.

In the first place the fairytale marriage of the young emperor to the young and beautiful Duchess Elisabeth of Bavaria, known as Sisi, had turned out to be anything but. From the day she arrived by boat in Vienna, Sisi had hated the formality and protocol of the imperial court. She did not get on with her domineering mother-in-law, and longed for the freedom of her childhood home, Possenhofen Castle, on the shore of Lake Starnberg in Bavaria.

Sisi was not one to bow to convention, however lofty. She had a mind of her own. She shocked her mother-in-law by having a gym installed in her apartment in the Hofburg Palace; she frequently indulged her passion for horses and riding; she insisted on preserving and exhibiting her beauty by combing her lustrous hair into which she set jewels, and having her ladies-in-waiting tie her into almost impossibly small-waisted dresses.* It was behaviour that bordered on the eccentric; certainly not to be expected of an empress.

She adhered to a strict diet. Meat disgusted her, so that a meal might consist of the juice of half-raw beef squeezed into thin soup, or a diet of just milk and eggs. She ate small amounts and very quickly, as if trying to avoid any long-term effect on her weight. If the smallness of her waist was in any way threatened, she would fast completely for several days. Today we would not hesitate to say she suffered from an eating disorder.

There is no question that her mental health was fragile, both genetically – there was inbreeding to the extent that her mother-in-law was also her aunt – and as an independent retaliation against a world she wished every minute of the day and night she had never joined.†

After her first child, Sophie, died at the age of just two, she refused to eat for days. As with Sophie, a second daughter was immediately taken away from her. Her mother-in-law refused to allow her to breastfeed or to have anything to do with the baby's care. Such treatment worsened her already erratic behaviour, leading to bouts of depression that consumed her for weeks.

Her husband, by contrast, was a simple soldier – his own description – with all a soldier's instincts for discipline,

---

* Known as 'tight-lacing'.

† In fact she had not been intended as the emperor's bride. His mother had chosen Elisabeth's elder sister, but Josef fell in love with Elisabeth and proposed to her.

obedience, an acceptance of duty and obligation. He was ill-equipped mentally to deal with a highly strung woman whose beauty was legendary throughout Europe, who made her own decisions about how and where to spend her time, and with whom.

Franz Josef indulged his wife in every way that he was capable of. When she developed a passion for Greece, he had a palace built for her on the island of Corfu. She rarely visited it.* When she announced that she was travelling to Britain and Ireland to go riding to hounds, he allowed it – refusing to listen to rumours that she was having an affair with the dashing Scottish horseman, Bay Middleton.

The Viennese, who had really wanted to love their empress, had long since realised that was an impossible wish. If anything, Elisabeth's eccentricities, which made life so difficult for her husband, increased the people's affection, even sympathy, for their emperor.

The empress was aware she was failing her husband in certain areas, and as if to confirm her unpredictable behaviour, somewhere around the mid-1880s she allowed her husband to take a mistress. A mistress chosen by the empress herself.

One evening in 1883 Franz Josef found himself in one of his least favourite places, the Burgtheater, that imposing building on the Ringstrasse where plays and opera were

---

* Today it is a museum to Empress Elisabeth owned by the Greek nation.

performed. The emperor was not a great theatregoer, in fact the arts in general were an area that rather passed him by. But on this occasion an actress by the name of Katharina Schratt had been engaged by the Imperial Hofburgtheater, and given the title 'Imperial and Royal Actress of the Burgtheater' (*Kaiserliche und Königliche Burg Schauspielerin*). It was customary when this happened for the actress (or actor) to thank the emperor personally for the honour.

And so Franz Josef, resplendent in military uniform, found himself talking to a tongue-tied young woman of thirty, twenty-three years younger than him. The oft-told story has the emperor imploring the young actress to sit, but she repeatedly refused. When finally he asked her why, she replied that she had been ordered to remain standing in his presence, at the risk of being expelled for lack of decorum.

Franz Josef is said to have laughed out loud so heartily that others waiting for an audience, as well as footmen and imperial staff, stood in astonishment. Never had anyone heard the normally stiff and reserved emperor let himself go quite like this.

In the months that followed, to general surprise, which gave way to mild amusement, Franz Josef developed an unexpected love of the theatre, attending more often than he had done for years.

Among those whose attention this behaviour had not escaped was the empress herself, and in Katharina Schratt she saw at least a partial solution to her marital problems.

She could see quite clearly that her husband had become infatuated with the young actress.

In a remarkable act of, shall we say, 'understanding', the empress decided that Katharina would make the ideal mistress for her husband. She had no aristocratic connections, therefore there could be no risk of political influence being sought. It was by no means unheard of for a ruler to take a mistress, and as long as the young woman could be persuaded to exercise at least a modicum of discretion, there would be benefit all round.

Empress Elisabeth's instinct told her Katharina was the right woman for the purpose, and in May 1886 she acted on that instinct. She decided to commission a leading artist to paint a portrait of Katharina. More than that, she invited her husband to come with her to the artist's studio to watch the painting in progress.

It appears Katharina was not let in on the empress's plan. Imagine the young actress, finding herself sitting for a society artist for a reason she was not aware of, suddenly finding herself in the company of the emperor and empress!

Franz Josef, clearly encouraged by his wife, lost no time in putting her plan into action. Two days after the visit to the artist's studio, the emperor sent Katharina an emerald ring to thank her 'for having gone to the trouble of posing for [the artist]'. In an extraordinarily affectionate note, he expressed his gratitude to her for sacrificing her time, and signed it 'your devoted admirer'.

Thus began a relationship that was to last until the end of the emperor's life thirty-four years later, and provide him over the years with succour and comfort through a series of tragic circumstances that he himself said no man should have to bear.* Given that, perhaps my earlier use of the word 'understanding' to describe the empress's action should be replaced by 'prescience'.

The first of these was an event so utterly traumatic and unexpected that it threatened the very fabric of the Habsburg monarchy. In the immediate chaos that followed, there were those who expected the dynasty itself, more than six hundred years old and destined to last for ever, to fall.

The seeds had been sown many years earlier by an event of unmatched happiness in the imperial capital.

After four and a quarter years of marriage, which had produced two daughters, one of whom had not survived, the empress set not just the city of Vienna, but the entire Habsburg empire, alight with joy by producing a son.

A 101-gun salute heralded the arrival on 21 August 1858 of an heir to the Habsburg throne, Archduke Rudolf, Crown Prince of Austria. The emperor's joy was complete.

---

* Katharina Schratt outlived the emperor by nearly twenty-four years, dying in 1940 at the age of eighty-six.

A son and heir, and a wife with her popularity restored, which would surely restore her own happiness.

It was a vain hope. The emperor's mother once again took control. If a daughter was not to be entrusted to its mother, how much less so was the son and heir to the throne. As the infant grew, Elisabeth was allowed to have no say over his upbringing or education.

Within two short years Elisabeth's health collapsed. She was only twenty-two years of age, but was suffering from such extreme physical exhaustion that tuberculosis was feared. Without a thought for court protocol, Elisabeth deserted the court, left her husband and children, and fled from Vienna.

She stayed away for six months, and within days of her return her health once more deteriorated. Elisabeth's health remained unstable in the years that followed. When she was away from Vienna, her health improved. As soon as she returned, she became ill again.

In August 1862, having been away from husband and children for two whole years, she returned to Vienna shortly before Franz Josef's birthday, but on the journey suffered from a violent migraine and vomited four times.

Without doubt we would say today that her illnesses were psychosomatic, but her physical reactions were certainly genuine. She hated Vienna, life at court, so much that she simply could not avoid falling ill.

This had one advantage. All the medical advice said that she was too fragile to risk another pregnancy. That at least released her from what her mother-in-law, and quite possibly poor Franz Josef, saw as her primary duty.

She herself was under no illusion over her priorities. A close confidante quoted her as saying, 'Children are the curse of a woman, for when they come they drive away beauty, which is the best gift of the gods.'

It is hardly surprising that the child on whom the future of the Habsburg dynasty depended was to grow up rather troubled. Taken from his mother at birth, then seeing so little of her that she was in effect a stranger, and taught the rigours and discipline of court life from as soon as he could stand.

If the infant rarely saw his mother, his relationship with his father was cold and formal. Franz Josef hardly knew how to bestow love on his son, other than in strict accordance with protocol. On the day the child was born his father had awarded him the Order of the Golden Fleece, and the following day appointed him Honorary Colonel-in-Chief of the 19th Regiment. Later he would promote him to Inspector General of the Infantry. One wonders if little Rudolf was ever cuddled by either mother or father.

Added to all this was the disturbing fact that his genetic provenance was, to say the least, fragile. His parents were first cousins, and both families were related several times over, with instances of mental illness on both sides.

It was as if Rudolf was destined for tragedy from the day he was born.

Thirty years later the heir to the throne was a disillusioned, even dangerous, young man. Where his father saw order and permanence, the son was certain that everything had to change. 'A tremendous change has to come,' he wrote to a friend, 'a social restructuring.'

The words were seditious. His thoughts were seditious. He mixed with the poor and anarchists. His behaviour verged on treason. He made no secret of his activities and allegiances; discretion was unknown to him. At the age of twenty he had written a twelve-page letter assessing the effects of military manoeuvres in Bosnia on the Slav people. Three months later he filled fourteen pages analysing the current political situation, with overt support for the growing movement for social democracy. It was not what you said in an empire where rule was by divine right, particularly when you yourself were heir to it.

Franz Josef simply did not know how to handle his rebellious son, and Empress Elisabeth was barely there to exercise any maternal influence. In fact she was in London, staying at Claridge's Hotel, when a telegram informed her of her son's engagement to a Belgian princess. It appears she had no idea of the proposed match until the telegram arrived.

With a profound belief that there could be no such thing as a happy marriage, proved by the disaster of her own, she is said to have turned white when she read it, and muttered, 'Please God it does not become a calamity.' She cannot have imagined just how far her prayer would go unanswered.

The emperor had taken matters into his own hands. His son and heir needed to settle down, have a family, start behaving like a normal young man in society, he decided. The chosen bride was Princess Stéphanie of Belgium. It was a perfect match, her mother being a Habsburg princess, thus uniting the two houses.

Perfect on paper, that was all. Stéphanie was a mere fifteen years of age, and the marriage, planned for the summer of 1880, had to be postponed for almost a year because it was found she had not yet begun to menstruate.

Archduke Rudolf, now twenty-two years of age, was not in the slightest bit attracted to his bride. After just a few weeks of married life, Stéphanie wrote that when she arrived from Belgium there were 'no plants, no flowers to celebrate my arrival, no carpets, no dressing table [in their rooms in Laxenburg Palace outside Vienna], no bathroom, nothing but a wash handstand on a three-legged framework'.

Of much more import, as it turned out, were her words that she and her husband had 'little to say to each other; we were virtual strangers'.

Around five years into the marriage Rudolf's health deteriorated sharply. He suffered from persistent bronchitis, coupled with rheumatic pains. He had constant headaches.

He started taking morphine, and soon became dependent on it. He was drinking too much alcohol as well.

And so we reach the year 1888, the year the emperor and his people were preparing to celebrate the fortieth anniversary of his accession to the throne. The actual date was 2 December.

In April that year Archduke Rudolf appeared to take total leave of his senses. Under a pen-name that fooled no one, he published a 15,000-word 'Open Letter to His Majesty Emperor Franz Josef I' on the subject of 'Austria-Hungary and its Alliances'. This was a son, heir to the throne, in open revolt against his father the emperor, just as preparations were being made for the anniversary celebrations.

But Franz Josef could not have known just how seriously unbalanced his son had now become. There was a sultry young dancer by the name of Mizzi Caspar, who had made herself well known, and available, to Rudolf and his officer friends. In the summer of this year he met her secretly and proposed that she should accompany him to the officers' memorial, which stood in the hills south of Mödling, close to Vienna.

She assumed it was for some kind of tryst. It was, he told her, but it was more than that. The monument bore an engraving 'To Emperor and Fatherland'. In front of it, he said, they would shoot themselves and die together. This concerned young woman laughed it off, telling him not to be so stupid and to come to his senses.

Then Rudolf met Mary Vetsera, the ambitious seventeen-year-old daughter of an ambitious mother. Ambitious for what? To enter the very highest aristocratic circles, and their prey was the heir to the throne. With her mother's overt encouragement, Mary set out first to become mistress to the archduke, then, who knows, maybe even succeed in displacing Princess Stéphanie.

But that was not the way it turned out. Mary succeeded in her first aim, but she became infatuated with Rudolf to such an extent that when he made the same suggestion to her that Mizzi had rejected, she saw it as her path to posthumous fame, even possible immortality.

There was one difference. Rudolf decided that their act of defiance against everything his father and the empire stood for would take place not in front of a memorial on the edge of a wood, but in the hunting lodge he had bought the year before in a village a little way to the southwest of Vienna, by the name of Mayerling.

While Rudolf hatched his devastating plan, Vienna celebrated. In fact the city had never celebrated like it. For the unveiling of a huge monument to the memory of the mother of the nation, Empress Maria Theresa, her arm outstretched as if to gather her people, the Prince of Wales was in Vienna, the King of Greece, the new Kaiser of Germany, all on show along with no fewer than sixty-six archdukes and archduchesses, there to pay respects, even homage, to the Habsburg emperor and his beautiful empress.

Only those standing close to Empress Elisabeth saw the

look of alarm on her face as she turned to her son. Rudolf was pale, deep shadows beneath his eyes. They heard her ask, 'Are you ill?' 'No, only tired and exhausted,' he replied.

On Monday, 28 January 1889, Crown Prince Rudolf and his mistress Mary Vetsera left separately for the fifteen-mile carriage ride to Mayerling. There was no secret about the trip, at least among those close to Rudolf. His father knew he was at Mayerling, and two close friends of Rudolf were there too, a prince and the court chamberlain, as well as a valet.

The following day the men went hunting, and in the evening they sat down to a hearty dinner. Mary stayed closeted in Rudolf's bedroom. Rudolf joined her there, with orders to be called at 7.30 a.m. for breakfast.

The next morning, after failing to get a response from inside the room, the drastic decision was taken to break down the door. Inside was a horrific scene. Mary Vetsera, fully dressed, was stretched out on the bed, hair flowing loosely, hands cupping a rose, blood already dried and caked from a gunshot wound to the temple.

Archduke Rudolf was half sitting on the bed, leaning against a night table on which stood a mirror, which had helped him perfect his aim. The blood was still flowing from his mouth. To even an untrained eye it was obvious what had happened: Rudolf had shot his mistress, and then *several hours later* turned the gun on himself.

In a single night the history of the Habsburg empire had changed.*

It was that interval of several hours that was the most problematic fact of all. This could not be passed off as a sudden act of folly, or desperation, the result of some traumatic quarrel. This was calculated, premeditated. Rudolf must have looked at the body of his mistress, the blood flowing from the head wound, slowly congealing, for several hours before himself committing suicide.

Not that that stopped the news being officially announced with every possible explanation except the true one. On one 'fact' every report agreed: there was only one body, that of Archduke Rudolf. To admit to two would cause all kinds of unseemly speculation.

The first report was that the Archduke had been poisoned by a jealous woman. When this was considered so unlikely as to be implausible, it was announced that Rudolf had died of a stroke. Another report said a heart attack was more likely in a man of thirty.

But it was impossible to suppress the truth. Almost. On 1 February the evening edition of the *Wiener Tagblatt* carried a black-framed monumental headline: THE MOST HORRIBLE TRUTH. It reported that Archduke

---

* It is not an exaggeration to say that the history of the world changed that night. The death of Rudolf made Archduke Franz Ferdinand, the emperor's nephew, heir to the Habsburg throne. It was his assassination in Sarajevo that was the catalyst for the outbreak of the First World War.

Rudolf had committed suicide by shooting himself in the head. He had, it said, been alone at the time.

Extraordinary measures were put in place to conceal the fact that Rudolf had not been alone, that a woman – never mind that it was his mistress – was with him, and had been shot by him in a suicide pact.

In scenes that are almost too macabre to be believed, two of Mary's uncles travelled in an unmarked carriage to Mayerling. They first identified their niece's body, then proceeded to wash caked blood from the body, after which they dressed it in coat and hat, boa, veil and shoes.

They stood Mary's corpse up, took an arm each, and walked her out under cover of darkness to the carriage. To use a hearse would have been out of the question. They lifted her into the carriage, forced her into a sitting position between them, with a broomstick pushed between her dress and her spine to keep her erect.*

Mary was buried quietly and secretly in the cemetery of a Cistercian monastery, the abbot allowing himself to be persuaded – no doubt with a substantial 'gift' to the monastery – that although suicide prevented a Christian burial, this case was different since the young woman concerned had suffered a 'temporary loss of her senses'.

Archduke Rudolf, by contrast, received the full panoply of Habsburg court mourning. He was laid out in state

---

* One report says, rigor mortis having set in, they needed to break one of Mary's legs in order to close the carriage door.

in his apartment at the Hofburg Palace, his body strewn with flowers, moustache elaborately waxed and combed, a large bandage covering his forehead and the entire upper part of his head.

Empress Elisabeth visited her son and kissed his lips. Her younger daughter, Archduchess Marie Valerie (known as Valerie), who accompanied her, gave an account of the scene, at the same time leaving us a witheringly accurate description of her brother's character:

> *He was so handsome and lay there so peacefully, the white sheet pulled up to his chest and flowers strewn all around. The narrow* [sic] *bandage on his head did not disfigure him – his cheeks and ears were still rosy with the healthy glow of youth – the restless, often bitter, scornful expression that was often characteristic of him in life had given way to a perfect smile. He never seemed so beautiful to me before – he seemed to be asleep and calm, happy.*

Hardly surprisingly the sudden death – and its manner – of the heir to the throne, and of a son who rarely saw his mother and did not get on with his father, did nothing to bring his parents any closer together.

It was Empress Elisabeth who was told the news first, initially complaining that she had given instructions that her daily Greek lesson should never be interrupted. She then told her husband. Significantly she did not attend

Rudolf's funeral, preferring to remain in prayer in a private chapel.

Also unsurprising, given what we know of their characters, is the different way in which each parent reacted to Rudolf's death. As a father Franz Josef grieved for his son, but the military bearing and discipline never wavered, at least in public. 'I bore up well,' he said after the funeral. 'It was only in the crypt that I could endure it no longer.'

There is no question that uppermost in his mind was the fact the heir to the Habsburg throne was now dead. What would that mean for the empire? Would it in any way weaken it? Would its enemies try to capitalise on the grave situation?

As for Elisabeth, she was riven with guilt. Not, it seems, for the fact she more or less deserted her son and had taken little interest in his upbringing or welfare, but for fear that she had passed on her family's mental instability – madness, not to put too fine a point on it – to her son.

If she believed what the Roman Catholic Church said, she had good reason to feel guilty. Like the Cistercian abbot, the pope himself had proved remarkably susceptible to inducements of one kind or another, finally allowing himself to be persuaded that Rudolf's suicide was not your normal suicide, but the consequence of 'a state of mental derangement', thus allowing Rudolf complete burial rites.

Rudolf thus suffered officially from mental derangement, and why might that be? His mother believed for the rest of her life that she at least bore some responsibility for that dreadful act on the night of 30 January 1889.

Rudolf's coffin took its place in the Imperial Crypt in the Augustinerkirche in the Neuer Markt in the centre of Vienna, where it would later be joined by those of his parents. They lie alongside each other to this day, closer in death than they ever were in life.

Vienna was in a state of shock. No living Viennese had known of such a portentous act. The nineteenth century had certainly been one of upheavals, and you only had to be in late middle age to have witnessed the street revolution of 1848 and the ignominious middle-of-the-night departure of the politician who had ruled with an iron fist, Klemens von Metternich.

There had already been one death in the imperial royal family. The emperor's brother, Archduke Maximilian, who had been installed on the throne of faraway Mexico, had been executed by firing squad in June 1867.*

There had been wars, both victories and defeats, even an economic crash. But of one thing it was possible to be absolutely sure: the Habsburg dynasty, secure for six hundred years, was immutable. An emperor died or abdicated, and his legitimate and rightful heir would

---

* He had done his duty, said the emperor, ever the military man.

succeed. This progression had come to a sudden and unnatural stop.

What no one could know, not the emperor himself nor his wife, was that the killing was not yet over. Another single and unnatural death would haunt Vienna, and the empire, within a few short years. And that in turn would be followed by more killing, on a hitherto unimaginable scale. It would run into millions.

But that lay ahead. For now, the people of Vienna who had celebrated the emperor's fortieth anniversary with such *élan*, found themselves thrown into the deepest mourning. And who, once again, did they turn to when in need of gaiety and laughter?

Why, the Waltz King, of course.

Chapter 17

The 'Emperor Waltz'

There are numerous photographs of Emperor Franz Josef, at least from middle age onwards, and dozens of painted portraits, facsimiles of which still hang in many a government office or hotel reception room today. They show the kindly visage, worn down by tragedy and the relentless unpredictability of events – 'Gentlemen, my hand is unlucky,' he once said to city officials, and that was before the final tragedy – but if you want a true character study of this longest serving of monarchs, *Der alte Herr* ('the Old Gentleman') to the people of his day and a century of succeeding generations, you need look no further than Johann Strauss the Younger.

In the autumn of 1889, the year following the fortieth jubilee of the emperor's reign, Strauss composed a new waltz entitled *'Hand in Hand'*. It was one of the pieces he intended performing in Berlin at a week of concerts, and the title was meant to echo a recent toast of friendship that Franz Josef had made to the German kaiser.

However, Strauss's Berlin publisher, Fritz Simrock* had the rather good idea that the piece should be renamed *'Kaiser-Walzer'* ('Emperor Waltz'), a title that could refer to either monarch, and thus be suitably flattering to both. He went ahead with his plan, published the piece under the new title, and thereby gave the world a single piece of music that many consider to be the finest, and at the same time most poignant, that Strauss ever composed.

The Swiss music critic William Ritter described the *'Emperor Waltz'* as symphonic, more tone-poem than dance, and 'the most beautiful flower the fantastic tree of Strauss's music has borne'.

The German dramatist and novelist Paul Lindau wrote to Strauss:

> *It is no exaggeration when I say that, in my musical view, nothing has been written since the days of Franz Schubert which, for pure melody and unspoiled beauty, can be compared with the first part of your* 'Kaiser-Walzer'. *In those [opening] bars there is more music, genuine, unadulterated music, than in many operas that last a whole evening but which leave the heart empty.*

---

* Grandson of Nikolaus Simrock, friend of Beethoven in Bonn, and founder of the music-publishing house that bears his name.

There certainly is. The opening is in fact a slow march. What is a march? Something boisterous, loud, noisy, to stamp booted feet to. Strauss's first stroke of genius is to mark the opening bars *pianissimo*, as quiet as possible. The effect is to make you lean forward, strain your ears, to catch what is being played.

These opening bars capture instantly the character of Emperor Franz Josef. He is a military man, but a quiet one. Not a soldier to stamp and shout, but one who quietly gives orders and is prepared to obey them with total discipline when required.

The German-born journalist and writer Heinrich Eduard Jacob, author of *Johann Strauss: A Century of Light Music*, described this opening passage as 'very discreet, which is not typical of Strauss', and adds:

> *Strauss possibly wrote nothing more beautiful – and nothing less like the Strauss as Vienna's dance enthusiasts conceived him – than this march, which excites by its very tranquillity.*

Strauss then lifts the volume slightly to *piano*, gives a foretaste of the beautiful waltz to come, then increases the volume more and more to a *forte*, bringing the entire orchestra in for a full-blown march.

But this does not last. It is as if the emperor himself is saying, 'No no, this is too public, too indiscreet, we must maintain our royal dignity.' A lone cello comes in, high in the upper register, with a theme so plaintive the emperor himself could be shedding tears.

With just solo cello sounding, the time changes to three-four, Strauss writes *Tempo di Valse* at the top of the score, and gives us the most heartrendingly beautiful waltz, with plunging intervals of an octave, a seventh, even a ninth. It is the sound, almost, of a sob, but as with everything about his subject, a controlled sob.

But why just one waltz, when two will do? And what a contrast the second waltz is. High violins and flute take the theme, with horns and oboe in counterpoint. This is the emperor remembering better days, when he was young and taking as his bride the most beautiful young duchess in Europe.

Memories, though, are painful for Franz Josef. A waltz like this cannot endure, and again it is high violins and flute that drift down, a melancholy phrase that does not so much end as peter out, as the first waltz comes back in, and we are once again in the emperor's private world, and once again *pianissimo*.

Back comes the second waltz, but still *pianissimo*, as though, try as he might, there can be no relief from the melancholia that sits on Franz Josef's shoulders. A brief passage played *fortissimo*, allowing him temporary respite, gives way to a new waltz, a descending phrase once more filled with sadness. At intervals musical laughter breaks out, but each time it is quickly stifled.

A third waltz now, and it is joyous. No matter what befalls him, Franz Josef refuses to surrender totally to despair. And back comes the march. The emperor on parade, inspecting his troops, relishing their respectful and admiring gaze.

And we are into yet a fourth waltz, pointed and even piquant, as Franz Josef enjoys a little humour with staff officers. But once again it is not allowed to last, as the very first waltz returns in an inverted version. Instead of the theme plunging huge intervals, it rises. But Strauss keeps hold of the reins, not allowing the sound to rise above *mezzo forte*.

Soon we are back into melancholia, and the first waltz with those plunging intervals, the controlled sobs once more, with the sound not rising above *piano*. Is the emperor wiping away tears as news reaches him of the tragedy at Mayerling?

Life must go on. A soldier's discipline will ensure he does not surrender. The march returns, as Franz Josef gratefully receives the enhanced love of his people, who want to share his pain at the loss of his son, their future emperor, in order to alleviate it if they possibly can.

Through the sadness of the first waltz, the emperor is determined to show his people that they have helped him come through the worst of times. Trombones and trumpets sound the martial notes that allow him to bestride the parade ground, his palace, the duties of state.

But he knows, they know, that in the end he will be overwhelmed by fate, by forces he cannot control. The march is abruptly cut off, and the lone voice of the cello returns, like a Cassandra with nothing to impart but prophecies of more tragedy to come.

And in the face of such predictions, the emperor behaves like any soldier – with defiance and dignity, a refusal to be cowed. So the music builds finally to a *fortissimo* finish. Nothing will break this man.

If I have taken a certain artistic licence in my descriptive analysis of the *'Emperor Waltz'*, one factor in Johann Strauss's life most certainly supports it. He knew the emperor well, and even if his intention had not been to create a portrait in music of the man, he must have realised how apt it was. Why else would he have agreed to the title being changed?

His role as Court Ball Director of Music brought him into frequent contact with the emperor and empress, even though they were hardly great concertgoers or aficionados of music. He was required to compose new pieces for special state occasions. For the emperor's diamond jubilee he composed the *'Kaiser-Jubiläum Jubelwalzer'* ('Jubilee Waltz for the Emperor's Jubilee'), which became instantly popular, even if it was to be rather eclipsed by the *'Emperor Waltz'*, which followed a year later.[*]

---

[*] In fact several Strauss biographies mistakenly state that the *'Emperor Waltz'* was specifically composed for the Jubilee.

It seems Johann Strauss knew the emperor on another level as well. The emperor's mistress, Katharina Schratt – Kathi to those close to her – was now fully accepted as part of his life. Should there be any doubt, the empress herself made a point of being seen both at court and in public together with her husband and Kathi, an overt declaration of her approval for what amounted to a *ménage à trois*.

For Kathi actually to take up residence in either the Hofburg or Schönbrunn Palace, though, would be considered a step too far, and so the emperor bought a villa for her in the Gloriettegasse, a secluded tree-lined street just outside the garden walls of Schönbrunn in Hietzing. Kathi was therefore on hand whenever the emperor was able to escape from his official residence in the centre of Vienna to the beautiful summer palace in Hietzing.

The wealthy suburb of Hietzing had both good, and not so good, memories for Strauss. It was where Dommayer's Casino stood, the venue that had seen his debut as conductor and composer nearly half a century earlier. It was also where he had lived contentedly with the wife he adored, Jetty, and where she had died.

We do not know under exactly what circumstances, but residents of Hietzing, well into the next century, spoke excitedly of the famous personages who frequented their district. It was said that the emperor himself would walk out of Schönbrunn Palace early of a summer's morning, stroll across to Kathi's villa, let himself in through the garden gate, and join his mistress for breakfast.

Johann Strauss, the locals said, often joined them, albeit later in the day. And do you know what the great composer liked to eat, they'd ask? Crayfish and goose-liver pâté, served with very dry champagne. Kathi always made sure she had it available to serve to him.

It's impossible to know exactly how much of this is true, though stories like that are usually founded on at least a modicum of truth. In fact only one conversation between Strauss and the emperor is actually authenticated, because it was witnessed by a number of people.

It took place on a glittering occasion. In 1894 Vienna celebrated the golden jubilee of Johann Strauss's career as a musician. It was fifty years since, as a nervous and apprehensive young man, he had stood in front of his orchestra at Dommayer's Casino, expressly against his father's wishes, and performed his first public concert.

Now, in his seventieth year, he was the object of veneration and admiration. A week of festivities was held in the city he had portrayed so many times in music, and the Viennese people, from lowest to highest, joined in the celebrations. The highest being the emperor himself.

The high point of the celebrations was a gala performance of Strauss's operetta *Der Zigeunerbaron*. To the surprise of the sophisticated audience in the Vienna State Opera, and to their delight, the emperor himself took his seat in the royal box.

Visits to the opera not being a regular feature of the emperor's duties, on the rare occasions when he did attend he would slip discreetly away during the second act. Since it was customary for the composer, or noted actor or singer (as with Katharina Schratt) to be presented to the emperor, this would happen during the first intermission, since by the end of the performance he would no longer be there.

As was usual, therefore, the theatre manager entered the royal box during the first intermission of *Der Zigeunerbaron* and asked the emperor if he wished to receive Johann Strauss immediately.

'No,' replied Franz Josef, 'I shall wait till the end and then I will receive Herr Strauss.'

To the surprise of his staff, and that of the theatre, he did as promised. During the thunderous applause that greeted the end of the performance, Johann Strauss was ushered into the royal box.

Franz Josef greeted him warmly. The emperor was in jovial mood and spoke loudly, words that were later recorded by one of his courtiers.

'I enjoyed myself immensely, Herr Strauss. You know it is strange, but your music ages as little as you do. You haven't changed at all in the long years I have known you. I congratulate you on your opera.'

What further words were uttered between the two men we do not know. But friends of Strauss, to whom he later relayed the experience, reported that one word, one particular word, had leapt out at him and caused him untold joy.

'Opera! The emperor said opera!' Probably unwittingly the emperor had paid Strauss the highest compliment he could.

If today we picture the encounter, we might well imagine one of them as elderly, with careworn face, balding, elaborate sideburns and moustache, somewhat stooped from personal cares and worrying matters of state, dressed in traditional military garb adorned with medals and sash, addressing a younger dark-haired individual, sprightly, darting eyes, nattily dressed, almost restless.

That is certainly how I see the emperor and Johann Strauss, and every word of my description is true, except one. *Younger*. Johann Strauss was five years older than the emperor.

Johann Strauss, perhaps surprisingly for a composer of such genial music, did not have many close friends. Despite appearances to the contrary, he was not a convivial man. He did not enjoy company, absented himself as much as he could from the occasions his profession obliged him to attend – necessary evils, as they were to him – and made as swift a departure as he could get away with.

His wife Adèle recognised this in him, and did all in her power to make sure he was content. She smoothed his path constantly, protecting him from outside influences that might cause him stress. A different kind of wife – Lili, for instance – might have bemoaned his lack of sociability, badgering him to allow her to arrange parties and soirées.

But not Adèle. She jealously guarded her husband's privacy at their house in the Igelgasse. Few people were allowed to cross the threshold who were not welcome visitors for her husband, and those who qualified were usually those with whom Strauss enjoyed a game of billiards or tarot, his favourite card game.

Alexander Girardi was one, the comic actor who brought so many of Strauss's characters to life on the stage.

Another was one of the most celebrated composers of his age, Johannes Brahms. Surprising though it may seem to us – indeed, surprising as it was to acquaintances of both men – a real friendship developed between them.

Two more contrasting individuals, both as men and musicians, would have been hard to find. Brahms was notoriously curmudgeonly, icily cold to those to whom he took a dislike. While Strauss certainly had a difficult side, when it was diplomatic to hide it he was able to do so. Brahms made no such effort.

Their music, too, was worlds apart. Brahms's works were deep, even dense, a musical commentary on philosophical issues that exercise the profoundest intellect. Not for nothing was he called Beethoven's natural successor. His works were intended to engage the mind.

Johann Strauss, by contrast, was a showman. He wrote music primarily to entertain. It was music to dance to, or music to accompany the absurdity of operetta plots on stage. Brahms, if you like, wanted his listeners to frown, while Strauss wanted them to smile.

So what brought these two composers together, made of them good friends and matchless admirers of each other's music? It is frankly impossible to explain, other than with clichés such as 'opposites attract'.

Certainly Adèle played a part. Both men clearly adored her, though obviously on different levels. Brahms, the inveterate bachelor, relished her company on a platonic level, never making either her or her husband feel uneasy in his company. On one occasion at a charity fête, a tambourine was purchased by one of the men. On it Brahms wrote, 'Service at the Court of Adèle' and beneath it, 'Brahms for fugues, Strauss for waltzes.'

On another occasion Adèle spotted Brahms in a restaurant. She went over to him and asked if he would sign a napkin for her. He took a pen, wrote out the opening bars of the *'Blue Danube'* waltz, and signed underneath, 'Alas not by Johannes Brahms' (*Leider nicht von Johannes Brahms*).*

Brahms was no mere flatterer when it came to his praise of Strauss's music. He would frequently sit at the piano and play the waltzes. The Hungarian composer Karl Goldmark once witnessed Brahms play the whole of *'By the Beautiful Blue Danube'* on the piano. He described how

---

* Other versions of this famous anecdote have Brahms signing Adèle's fan, or a score of *'By the Beautiful Blue Danube'*.

Brahms played an improvisation of the introduction, and then proceeded to produce a 'marvel of spontaneous evolution of the musical material'.

Both Strauss and Brahms had a favourite destination that they would go to in the summer to get away from the oppressive heat of Vienna – Strauss on the advice of his doctor to counter bouts of illness. It was the beautiful spa town of Bad Ischl, some 170 miles south-west of Vienna, on the edge of the Salzkammergut mountain range, which stretches east from Salzburg across Upper Austria.

Both men had villas on the same slope leading up from the crystal-clear waters of the River Traun.* On the other side of Bad Ischl, on a wooded rise, was the grand summer palace given to young Franz Josef as a wedding present from his mother. He loved to spend time there, describing it as 'heaven on earth'. Sisi rarely, if ever, went there – it held too many bad memories. In her eyes it represented the beginning of her 'enslavement' as a member of the imperial royal family.

The palace was conveniently placed for the emperor. A short walk along the river, through a gate, and he was inside a villa that his mistress Kathi Schratt had acquired. The convenience was mutual. Kathi was given a key to the emperor's villa – by Sisi herself. A photograph taken in 1910, when the emperor was eighty years of age and Kathi

---

* The house Brahms rented is still there. On the site where Strauss's villa stood there is now an unprepossessing modern apartment block.

approaching fifty-seven, shows them walking as a couple in the grounds of the imperial villa in Bad Ischl.

The emperor, in dark military uniform with resplendent whiskers, looks weighed down by matters of state. His mistress, in smart suit, fur stole round her shoulders, stylish hat, parasol in right hand, is talking to him. It looks as though she, a retired actress who left her youth and looks long behind, is counselling him, offering advice to this man who had ruled his empire for more than sixty years. Not for nothing was she known as 'the uncrowned Empress of Austria'.

Johannes Brahms and Johann Strauss spent many a summer month in Bad Ischl, often planning their visits so they would be there at the same time. It is not known whether either of the composers met the emperor in Ischl, though it seems more than likely. What is known is that towards the end of his life, Brahms would stroll to the elegant Café Zauner to join Kathi Schratt for tea and pastries.

Strauss delighted in playing ideas to Brahms on the piano, and they chatted and drank for many an hour. Proof of just how comfortable these two great musicians, two such different individuals, were in each other's company is another photograph, this one earlier than that showing Franz Josef and Kathi, taken in September 1894.

It shows Strauss and Brahms standing on the veranda of Strauss's villa. Brahms, on the right, has receding grey hair exposing a high domed forehead and a full snowy white beard falling to his chest. He is heavily built – grossly overweight in today's terms.

His all-black suit is shapeless. His black shoes are dull and unpolished. The only concession to anything not black is a gold or silver watch chain. His left arm is stretched onto the balcony balustrade, causing his jacket – already several sizes too long, reaching almost to his knees – to fall open and appear several sizes too big.

What a contrast Johann Strauss provides! Dark dyed-black hair swept luxuriantly back, neatly trimmed black moustache, his clothes looking as if they might have come straight off a showroom mannequin. Stylish dark jacket, immaculately creased black-and-white-checked trousers, dark waistcoat, white winged-collar shirt with flamboyantly knotted silver tie, shoes polished like mirrors.

He has a trim figure, with not an ounce of spare flesh on him. His left arm is also on the balcony balustrade, but casually bent at the elbow, matching the left leg seductively bent at the knee.

Neither man is smiling, but I am ready to bet that if Strauss's upper lip were not entirely hidden by his moustache, it would reveal a suppressed smile.

As with Strauss and the emperor, if you were challenged to put an age to each man, you could quite easily say that Brahms was around seventy years of age, whereas Strauss might be somewhere around fifty, quite possibly even in his late forties.

When the photograph was taken, Johannes Brahms was

sixty-one years and four months, whereas Johann Strauss was just one month short of his sixty-ninth birthday!

Another photograph taken the following year shows Strauss at work on the same veranda of his house in Bad Ischl. There is the tall desk that he liked to stand at to compose, which befitted his restless nature. Manuscript papers are on the desktop, a pen is in his right hand. The forearm of his bent left arm rests on the desktop. This time the anxious look is back on his face.*

The picture is totally posed. One can almost hear the photographer telling him to try to relax, to bend the left knee, rest the left arm on the desktop. Equally I am sure Strauss is muttering under his breath, 'Just hurry up and be done with it. I have work to do.'

Johann Strauss at work was a very different individual from the man relaxing with his good friend Johannes Brahms.

Despite his youthful appearance, age was taking its toll on Johann Strauss. Always with an edgy, difficult side to his character, now as he approached seventy he had no need to hide or curb it. He was world famous; his compositions were adored across continents. He hobnobbed with royalty. If he wanted to be difficult, unsociable, who was to tell

---

* See plate section, page 3.

him not to be? Most certainly not his wife, who was more than content to indulge her famous husband.

If this side to his character was now exhibited in public, what did it matter? He could survive anything that his detractors might say against him. And some of them had very harsh things indeed to say.

The Viennese newspaper *Die Presse*, unimpressed with the elaborate celebrations of Strauss's golden jubilee, made its views known in unrestrained language:

> *Strauss is nervy and a hypochondriac. He has every possible and impossible illness, especially suffering from the same malady as some acquaintance who has just died. In actual fact, there is nothing wrong with him. But one is never quite as ill as when one is suffering from an illness one doesn't have.*

Die Presse was at least partly right. Strauss was a hypochondriac, and always had been. His brother Josef had practically accused him to his face of feigning illness during his trips to Russia all those years ago.

But as old age crept over him, there is no doubt that his health did actually suffer. Always with the caveat that any kind of retrospective diagnosis more than one and a quarter centuries after the event is fraught with danger, a doctor today might well find on examining him that Strauss suffered from neuralgia, arthritis, chronic bronchitis and influenza.

But there was quite possibly more to it than physical ailments. Beginning in 1983 the Austrian musicologist and Strauss specialist, Professor Franz Mailer, published ten annotated volumes of Strauss family letters and documents over almost thirty years. He wrote, 'Many signs lead one to infer [that Johann Strauss suffered from] severe psychiatric illness.'

Contemporary accounts are similar. The author Ignaz Schnitzer, who wrote the libretto for *Der Zigeunerbaron* and therefore worked closely with Strauss, relates how Strauss's mood could suddenly, and dangerously, change:

> *Morose, unspeaking, hardly looking up, he would skulk for days or weeks on end unsociably around the house, or keep himself cocooned in his work room. His own wife hardly dared to speak to him then, since to be disturbed in this ill-humoured silence could bring him to furious agitation.*

In the last decade of his life Strauss would spend the summers in Bad Ischl, the winters at his house in the Igelgasse. While he enjoyed the warm scented air in the Salzkammergut, in the city during winter he would complain of pain and tiredness and more or less confine himself to his room. Both in Bad Ischl and Vienna he continued his habit of composing mostly at night, as he had told the American journalist in New York many years before. Beside his work desk in the Igelgasse house was a bell, which he rang to summon Adèle at any hour of the night to hear a new tune he had created.

Inevitably his nocturnal habits affected his eyesight, and increased his overall melancholy. In October 1894, just days after his golden-jubilee celebrations, he wrote to his brother Eduard:

> *I see everything double. If I take a toothpick, I always see two before me. If I should have the misfortune to go blind, I shall shoot myself. Of all physical ailments, this is the most insurmountable. Not to read – [or] be able to write, would take away from me all joy of life.*

Alongside Johann's obsessive fear of death, he also developed a phobia of disease and avoided anything that could bring him into contact with it. One of these possible sources of illness was Adèle's daughter Alice. Johann adored her as if she were his own child, but he strictly forbade her to invite her friends into his house for fear of catching some childhood ailment from them.

Of one fact Johann Strauss was acutely aware, and it was unique to him among composers. Strauss owed more to the city of his birth, Vienna, than he could ever repay. No great composer of the nineteenth century had rooted his music so firmly in the city of his birth.

As I have already noted, only one other truly great musical name of the nineteenth century was actually born in Vienna, as opposed to moving to live there, and that was

Franz Schubert. Describe Schubert's music in any way you wish, but to call it typically Viennese would be wrong. It is typically Schubertian.

Strauss's music alone distils the essence of Vienna into musical notes, and he knew it. At the festival banquet held at the Grand Hotel in Vienna for his golden jubilee, in the company of two hundred people, including composers, writers and artists, he responded to a toast in his honour with these words:

> *If it is true that I have some talent, then I have to thank for its development my dear native city of Vienna, in whose earth my whole strength is rooted, in whose air lie the sounds which my ear gathers, which my heart takes in and my hand writes down ... Vienna, the heart of our beautiful, God-blessed Austria ... to her I give my cheer: Vienna, bloom, prosper and grow!*

Vienna was not to obey his command. The city, the country, the empire, was heading inexorably towards oblivion. Johann Strauss would not live to witness that. But he would live to see the next great personal tragedy unfold, a tragedy so profound and unexpected that Emperor Franz Josef, on being informed, would visibly shrink and age.

'Am I then to be spared nothing?' the emperor would ask, trying with all the military discipline he could muster to contain his grief.

Chapter 18

An Assassin's Knife Breaks the Emperor's Heart

In one of those quirks of history, two men whose names were previously unknown would soon enter the story of the Habsburg empire. The second of these, whom I will address later, would fire a volley of shots that would kill two people, and lead to the deaths of millions. The first would wield a stiletto knife, kill a single person, and bring a man already tortured with pain and regret to unknown despair.

The name Luigi Luccheni is forgotten to history, but for a brief moment in September 1898 it was emblazoned across the newspapers of the world. Born in Paris to Italian parents, he grew up as an orphan, working later as labourer and bricklayer, then as a cavalry officer's servant. At some stage in young adulthood he became an anarchist, joined the extremist 'Regicide Squad', and set himself the task, or was assigned the task by colleagues, of assassinating a member of European royalty, a 'great deed' from which the monarchies of Europe would not recover. The chosen target was Prince Henri of Orléans, pretender to the throne of France. The prince was known to be intending to visit Geneva, and so Luccheni based himself there.

Several hundred miles north of Geneva, in central Germany, the Empress of Austria was in the spa town of Bad Nauheim enjoying a rest and buying presents for her grandchildren. Actually, 'enjoying' is not entirely the right word. Her daughter Archduchess Marie Valerie, who had been with her for two weeks in Bad Ischl, described her as being 'in low spirits, as always'. Bad Ischl had that effect on her.

Valerie sided with her mother and largely blamed the emperor for 'the melancholic effect of court life, this exclusion from all natural situations ... What sort of life must Papa lead if he finds life here comfortable and enjoyable?'

Sisi then left for Switzerland, travelling incognito and accompanied only by a close friend and lady-in-waiting Countess Sztáray. Under the pseudonym of Countess von Hohenembs, she and her friend checked into the Hotel Beau Rivage on the shores of Lake Geneva.

The hotel manager, though, knew perfectly well who she was, and boasted to the local newspaper of his distinguished guest. The following morning the paper carried an item saying that the Empress of Austria was staying at the Beau Rivage in Geneva.

Luccheni the anarchist was in some despair. At the last minute Prince Henri had cancelled his trip to Geneva. What was he to do now? Would there be no 'great deed'? In despair he picked up a copy of the local newspaper, and the empress's fate was sealed.

Sisi had recently developed a fondness for Switzerland (no royal family, therefore no formalities or protocol), and her mood improved markedly. On Saturday, 10 September, she and her friend sat down to an early lunch in the hotel, enjoying first tea and patisseries and then a three-course lunch, which included a half-bottle of Médoc. The hotel bill, which includes the lunch (and, it appears rather extraordinarily, lunch the following day for six people), is quite clearly made out in the name of 'Madame la Comtesse de Hohenembs'.

Afterwards they walked the short distance to the landing stage on the banks of Lake Geneva to take the 1.40 p.m. lake steamer to Montreux. Sisi was dressed entirely in black, wearing a full-length dress with long embroidered sleeves and high-ruffed collar, cinched tightly at the waist. She carried a parasol in one hand and fan in the other.

Luccheni had hidden in his right sleeve a long thin file which he had ground to a sharp edge, set into a large round wooden handle with a strap so that he could hold it securely.

As the two women approached the landing stage Luccheni ran up to them, ducked under Sisi's parasol, paused to make sure he could locate her left breast (a book of anatomical drawings in his room had shown him exactly where the heart was found), and then plunged the file into her chest. He withdrew it quickly and hurried off.

Sisi temporarily lost her balance, but quickly recovered and said to her friend, 'What did that man want? Maybe he wanted to take my watch.' She assured her friend that she was all right, and the two women covered the short distance to the stage to board the steamer.

They stood on deck as the steamer departed. Suddenly Sisi let out a small sigh and collapsed to the floor. The countess thought she had fainted and began to unbutton the bodice of the dress. Only then did she notice a small tear in the dress and a brownish stain on the camisole underneath it.

She called out to the captain to come quickly, informed him who her mistress was, and asked him to return to shore as swiftly as he could. Once the boat docked Sisi was laid on an improvised stretcher made up of oars and velvet chairs, and carried as quickly as possible back to the hotel.

A doctor was summoned, and although Sisi was still breathing faintly he was able to ascertain that she had moments only to live. He explained to the countess that Sisi had survived as long as she had only because the weapon used was so narrow and the wound so small that the heart continued to beat and only gradually slowed as the flow of blood increased.

The dress she was wearing has been preserved, I have seen it. The tear above the heart is so small it is not at all surprising that she was not immediately aware of what had happened.

Empress Elisabeth was sixty years and nine months when she died, and those closest to her found consolation in the knowledge that death had come to her as she had wanted – swiftly and without warning.

Her daughter Valerie remembered that her mother had said, 'Let death take me unawares. And when it is time for me to die, lay me down at the ocean's shore,' and after she received news of her mother's death, she wrote, 'Now it has happened as she always wished it to happen, quickly, painlessly, without medical treatment, without long, fearful days of worry for her dear ones.'

In the Hofburg Palace in Vienna the emperor had written a letter that morning to Kathi saying, 'The empress is enjoying the pure, invigorating mountain air of Switzerland.' At half past four in the afternoon an adjutant came in clutching a telegram. He said there was bad news from Geneva, the empress had been 'injured'.

The emperor, who without doubt had always loved his wife, even if he had been at a loss to understand her erratic behaviour, was endlessly concerned about her fragile health. He barely had time to wonder at the use of the word 'injured', before a second telegram arrived minutes later with the news of her murder.

Franz Josef, who had already lost his brother to a firing squad and his eldest son to suicide, had now lost the woman he fell so completely in love with all those years ago to an assassin. The adjutant reported that the emperor turned away and muttered almost under his breath, 'So I am to be spared nothing in this world.' (*'Mir bleibt doch gar nichts erspart auf dieser Welt.'*) And then, even more quietly, 'Nobody will ever know how much we loved each other.' (*'Niemand weiss, wie sehr wir uns geliebt haben.'*)

As for the assassin, he had what he wanted – his moment in the spotlight. He was chased and wrestled to the ground by hotel staff who were carrying the two women's bags. A photograph was taken of him being led away by two gendarmes. He strides along, arms swinging, a smile of satisfaction on his face, a gondolier's hat set at a jaunty angle on his head. He was tried, convicted, and sentenced to life imprisonment. Eleven years later, in 1910, he hanged himself in his cell.

Luccheni had indeed murdered a royal personage, but in his prime objective he had failed totally. The emperor and his people were in mourning, but Sisi's death did not affect the constitutional affairs of the Habsburg empire one jot. It might even be something of an exaggeration to say that the people were in mourning. A confidant of the emperor, who was also Governor of Lower Austria, said, 'Not many tears were shed for her.'*

---

* Even if this was true, it was a short-term reaction. A trilogy of films on the empress's life starring Romy Schneider, made in the 1950s, remains popular to this day, and on the centenary of the empress's death in 1998 several new biographies were published, and Sisi's portrait adorned hundreds of shop windows in Vienna.

If the final decade of the nineteenth century seemed to offer nothing but heartache for Emperor Franz Josef, the same was true – surprising though it may seem – on a professional level for Austria's best-loved and most famous composer.

We know Johann Strauss the younger today as the composer of the waltz *sans pareil*. He was the undisputed master of the form. The names of his greatest waltz pieces echo down the years and will continue down the centuries: *'The Emperor Waltz', 'By the Beautiful Blue Danube', 'Tales from the Vienna Woods', 'Wine, Woman and Song', 'Voices of Spring', 'Vienna Blood', 'Roses from the South'.*

But the urge to be a great composer of opera never left him. Failing that, well, to be known first and foremost as a composer of operetta would do nicely. Putting this desire into the context of its time, it is perhaps not too difficult to understand the ambition.

This was the era of Wagner and Verdi. The operas of both composers were sweeping across Europe. Wagner had his detractors, but few doubted he was rewriting the musical rule book. No one had written operas like his; no one had created harmonies such as his.

Verdi was entirely different. Instantly memorable tunes, so much so that in the case of one of them – *'La donna è mobile'* – he forbade his performers to whistle it in the street ahead of opening night, for fear of it becoming known too soon.

Certainly there were composers of the nineteenth century who had established themselves firmly in musical history without ever having written an opera, or in the case of Beethoven just one. As well as Beethoven, there were names such as Schubert, Mendelssohn, Schumann, Bruckner, Brahms, Mahler – symphonists, first and foremost, all of them.

To attend a concert was an activity that belonged largely to the cultured classes. While the same might be true of Wagner, it was very different in the case of Verdi in Italy, Offenbach in France, or Gilbert and Sullivan in Britain. The theatre was entertainment in a way that a purely musical performance could not be. And the theatre belonged to everyone.

The music that Johann Strauss wrote fell, to some extent, between the two *genres*. It could most certainly be played at a concert, but it was better in a dance hall or even in a café. It was music that needed to be moved to. Although performers could dress in traditional costume and dance on stage in front of an audience, it was not by any stretch of the imagination opera.

And so, while he was producing immortal waltzes, polkas, even marches and quadrilles, he still longed for recognition as a composer of stage works. Proof of this is that in a thirty-one-year period, from 1868 to his death in 1899, Strauss composed no fewer than seventeen stage works – sixteen operettas and one opera. The number is nineteen, if you include the two false starts. That might be fewer than Verdi, but it is more than Wagner.

Of that number only one, *Die Fledermaus*, remains firmly in the repertoire to this day, with occasional outings for *Eine Nacht in Venedig* and *Der Zigeunerbaron*. That means sixteen failures or near failures, which Strauss found very hard to deal with. He went on trying to recreate the success of *Die Fledermaus* right up until his death.

By the beginning of the 1890s, the final decade not just of the century but of Johann Strauss's life, he had composed twelve operettas. In the nine years left to him, one opera and four more operettas would follow.

They would prove a succession of failures to some degree or other, and it is not an exaggeration to say that, given his nervous disposition, ailments real and imaginary, they would exacerbate his health problems and even hasten his death.

The first of these was his only opera, and he knew even before he had written a single note that it was destined for failure, despite encouragement from his good friend Johannes Brahms.

Ritter Pásmán was a convoluted medieval tale about an unchivalrous kiss, adapted from a Hungarian poem by a lawyer, diplomat and journalist who was also a playwright. Johann had begun work on it in early 1888, but soon got bogged down.

As always when work was difficult, his health suffered,

and he took himself off to the spa town of Franzensbad to take the waters, as well as mud-bath treatments for gout and neuralgia.

By August 1891 he was thoroughly dispirited. He was in dispute with his publisher, whom he accused of making unreasonable demands and deliberately withholding a contract, and the constant need for rewriting and revision was wearing him down. He wrote to a friend:

> *Nothing comes of writing operas ... So much torment, so many false temptations in the inventing of melodies ... By the time I have finished trips to the spa, two full months will have passed without a note being written ... I cannot but confess that my heroic decision to write an opera not infrequently fills me with despair.*

After the final rehearsal, Johann was heard to say, 'I have heard it just as I had imagined it. The public can make of it what they will.'

And they did. The critics for the most part were unkind, and although there were initially full houses, *Ritter Pásmán* disappeared from the repertoire of the Court Opera after just nine performances. It fared little better in Prague, Dresden or Munich.

Johann was a composer of dance music, whether he liked it or not, and he knew it. The following April, when it was clear the opera would not be revived, he confessed with some bitterness to his brother Eduard, 'I only wrote it to prove that I can do more than write dance music.' And he added cynically that given the amount of corruption in society, maybe the opera would have done better if instead of just a misplaced kiss, the king had gone the whole hog and bedded the knight's wretched lady.

Ritter Pásmán was Johann's first and last attempt at opera. But he had not given up on operetta.

A year later his new operetta premiered, and if this too ultimately failed, the blame can at least to some extent be laid at the feet of Johann himself. He blamed everybody except himself, and it was almost as if he willed the operetta to fail. *Fürstin Ninetta* ('Princess Ninetta') was a comedy, written by a well-established team of comedy writers.

Johann was not impressed:

> *[This is] the most miserable libretto ever perpetrated ... I write at this piece of work without inspiration – it will be a real piece of rubbish.*

And it is clear where his real ambition still lay:

> *I shall still succeed in getting people to say, 'He ought to write operas.' That would be a triumph!*

Later he complained that he had not been given the whole libretto, including dialogue, so had had to work from lyrics alone. This caused an outburst of vitriol and cynicism which says a lot about Johann's state of mind:

> *The music is completely unsuited to this senseless, inar-*
> *tistic stuff ... It is a piece of fancy footwork around the*
> *author's jokes! ... I would be even happier if the entire*
> *thing were soon committed to a geriatrics' home. They*
> *can steal it from me, I shall not shed a tear over it.*

This is Johann Strauss the angry man, bitter, dissatisfied with being lauded the world over for his waltzes, wanting above all to be admired on the same level as a Verdi or a Wagner. It is also a man who, at sixty-seven years of age, is in declining health, imagining himself to be in worse health than he actually is, which increases his depression, even – extraordinarily – his lack of self-esteem as a composer.

Fürstin Ninetta was in fact a success at its premiere on 10 January 1893, and no one was more surprised than the composer himself. The critics, though, were once again un-kind. One in particular, in the periodical *Hans Jörgel*, cut Johann to the quick:

> *Sadly, Maestro Strauss has grown old. The dazzling*
> *giant reflector of his rich musical inventiveness is no*
> *longer functioning. His newest work reminds one of*
> *so-called 'official city illuminations'. Everything thor-*
> *oughly neat and very tidy, but without inner vitality,*
> *without breathtaking melodies.*

It might just as well have added: 'Stick to what you know best, Herr Strauss. Stick to waltzes.'

It is small wonder that Johann continued to lambast the piece as a 'scatterbrained, bombastic tale'. Small wonder too, that if the composer himself would not get behind it – and a composer as highly respected as Strauss – there was no hope for it. In fact *Fürstin Ninetta* ran for a very respectable seventy-six performances at the Theater an der Wien, before joining its predecessors in relative obscurity.

Three more operettas followed in the next three years, and as before, Johann was jinxed with poor librettos, ill health and his own seemingly fathomless pessimism.

The timing of the next one could not have been more critical. Johann chose a Slavonic subject set in Serbian south Hungary during the annual Apple Festival, when young men gathered to choose their bride. The operetta was to be called *Jabuka* ('The Apple Festival'). Johann was in buoyant mood. He began work on the piece in early May 1893 and predicted he would complete it by the end of the year.

But once again his demons intervened. It was almost as though once again he wanted it to fail. No sooner did he begin work than he began to suffer agonising attacks of 'head neuralgia' and bronchial catarrh. He told his brother Eduard that such debilitating illnesses were preventing him 'conquering this giant work'.

He also complained – again – about the librettists, two this time, which made the whole process doubly difficult. 'Each one wants to correct the other, with the upshot that there is no improvement.'

Inevitably he fell behind, causing anxiety to the theatre,

not to mention the singers who had been engaged. It became clear that the opening night would have to be postponed. Just how depressed Johann had become with the whole project shows clearly in a note he sent to the theatre agent and publisher who had acquired the rights to the operetta. This is literally gallows humour with, I suspect, more than an underlying layer of truth:

> *Save yourself the weeping and wailing for later … If* [Jabuka] *does not succeed, we can hang ourselves next to one another … just as long as I can see you swinging before I pull the rope around my own neck.*

I said timing was critical. Who knows, perhaps if the premiere had not taken place when it did, that gallows humour might have become a reality. *Jabuka* opened at the Theater an der Wien on 12 October 1894, just one day before Johann was guest of honour at the Vienna Court Opera at the start of celebrations for his golden jubilee.

Two weeks of festivities followed, during which Johann was lauded as Vienna's most famous musical son. There was no time to brood on a failure. Actually, once again *Jabuka*, like its immediate predecessors, was not exactly a failure. The *Neue Freie Presse* described the opening night as 'electrifying, especially the second and third acts [which] caused a sensation'. *Hans Jörgel*, which seemed to have it in for Johann, reported that the second-night audience responded 'much more coolly'.

Jabuka achieved fifty-seven performances in its first year, which might not be a staggering success but is far from being a failure. But then it dropped entirely out of the repertoire, and Johann chalked it up as another failure.

But he still wasn't giving up. Another two operettas followed in the next three years. They found perhaps their greatest advocate in Johann's good friend Johannes Brahms. The great composer was in failing health, but he championed the first, *Waldmeister* ('Woodruff'), and despite being largely bedridden attended the premiere of the second, *Die Göttin der Vernunft* ('The Goddess of Reason'). Brahms died just three weeks later, never to know that neither of the two operettas would remain in the repertoire.

Brahms did better than his friend. Johann was too ill to attend the premiere of *Die Göttin der Vernunft*. He had another attack of bronchial catarrh – why does this not come as a complete surprise? – but arranged to have news of how the audience was reacting telephoned through to his home at the end of each act.

He will have known, therefore, that the audience did not exactly leap to their feet. A kindly critic, writing for *Fremdenblatt*, put this down to their disappointment on learning that Johann was too ill to attend, which dampened their mood. A less kindly, and more realistic, critic in the *Neue Freie Presse* asked how you could possibly expect a burlesque comedy set amid the turmoil and cruelty of the

French Revolution to succeed. 'Can you disguise a blood-red guillotine with flowers?' his review asked.

Johann, finally, was finished with operetta. As a composer of opera, he had failed. As composer of operetta he had had one extraordinary success, two moderate successes, and a succession of failures. It was time now for one more attempt to prove he could do more than write waltzes and polkas, one more attempt to prove himself a 'serious' composer.

So what did he do? He turned his hand to ballet.

You really cannot avoid the feeling that Johann was rather pushed into composing a ballet. It seems the idea came from the highly influential music critic Eduard Hanslick, known as Vienna's 'music pope'.*

Hanslick organised a competition inviting writers and librettists to submit a text, which Johann Strauss would then set to music to produce a ballet. The entries would be judged by a distinguished panel of musicians, including – naturally – himself, as well as the man whose inclusion probably persuaded Johann Strauss to take part, a man he greatly admired, the artistic director of the Vienna Court Opera, Gustav Mahler.

Hanslick and his fellow judges were totally taken aback

---

* Hanslick's 1854 publication *The Beauty in Music* was hugely influential. An early supporter of Wagner, his enthusiasm for him, as well as Liszt, and 'the music of the future', cooled. He is believed to have influenced Brahms's music, and dismissed Tchaikovsky's Violin Concerto as putting the audience 'through hell' with music which 'stinks to the ear'.

by the response. By May 1898 no fewer than 700 entries had been received. The winner was adjudged to be one A. Kollmann from Salzburg, who submitted a modern version of the *Cinderella* story.*

Johann Strauss then set to work and a familiar pattern unfolded. At first he threw himself into the project, but it was not long before tedium, coupled with his natural pessimism, overtook him. He wrote to brother Eduard:

> *I have my hands full with the ballet. I am writing my fingers to the bone, and still make no headway. I am on the 40th sheet (full score) and have only managed 2 scenes.*

By late autumn Johann had completed the first draft of the ballet, which was called *Aschenbrödel* ('Cinderella'). He interrupted work on it to conduct just the overture at a special matinee performance of *Die Fledermaus* at the Vienna Court Opera House on 22 May 1899, to mark the traditional springtime holiday.

Why only the overture, as opposed to the whole work? All his life Johann had been ambivalent towards conducting. First Josef, then Eduard, had taken on the conducting while he got on with composition – to him a much more worthwhile pursuit.

---

* The name was soon discovered to be a pseudonym, and to this day the writer's real identity has not been uncovered.

This gives the lie to the thousands of images and statu-
ettes we have today of Johann Strauss, violin in one hand,
bow raised high in the other, one hip cocked, one knee
bent, a trance-like smile of happiness etched on his face as
he leads his orchestra. It might be an exaggeration to say
he hated directing the orchestra, and more truthful to
say he did it because he knew he had to. When, sometime in late middle age, he began to suffer from arthritis
and could no longer play the violin, he happily swapped it
for the baton. He would just as happily have given that
up too.

A letter he wrote to Eduard made it clear that it was his
health, once again, that was dictating his musical career:

> *On account of my health I must, as much as possible,
> keep away from conducting … because at the end
> of a number I leave the orchestra as if bathed in
> sweat, and unlike another person I cannot simply
> change my underclothes. I have to stay in the same
> attire for 5–6 hours, until the soaked outfit dries out
> by itself.*

His compromise, in later years, was to agree to conduct
the overture alone then hand the baton to a conductor
who would take over for the rest of the performance. As
far as we know, the last time Johann conducted an entire
operetta was the 200th performance of *Die Fledermaus* at
the Theater an der Wien on 15 May 1888.

Now, eleven years later almost to the day, he agreed to conduct the overture to his most popular and beloved work at the Vienna Court Opera House. It was not only to be the last time he would conduct, but the last time he would appear in public.

Chapter 19

A Final Fledermaus *and Johann Strauss Bids Farewell*

Those who were there said Johann Strauss conducted the overture to *Die Fledermaus* with a vigour and intensity they had not seen before, as if somehow he knew it would be the last time.

They were, of course, speaking with the benefit of hindsight. But I imagine the eyes blazing, sweat already breaking out on his forehead in nervous anticipation, perhaps a last run of the left hand through the hair, before bringing the baton down for the rising notes that begin the orchestral swell.

A brisk twelve-bar introduction of runs and triplets that come to rest in a single held note. Some soft *staccato* chords and an oboe soars above. The violins take over, there's a long *crescendo*, and then *fortissimo* the violins rise, syncopated chords, and we are into the first theme taken from the operetta itself, into a second theme, and already the audience is swaying to melodies that are so well known, not just across Vienna and Europe, but the world.

What is going through Johann's mind? Is he asking himself why he was never able to repeat the success of this, his best-loved operetta? He has little time to contemplate, as *staccato pianissimo* notes in violins and cellos lead without a pause straight into the first waltz, which with its turning phrase and firm end notes seems to distil the essence of Vienna, a tune beloved of whistling *fiacre* drivers, as they gently gird their decorated horses into a trot.

The waltz repeats itself, this time *forte* for good measure, before leading straight into a second waltz, which springs high to the top of the E string for the first violins. And yet a third waltz, to which the audience hums along, smiling at the familiarity.

A march then, to which the characters will soon be stomping across the stage. We are already at Prince Orlofsky's ball, where all the masked chicanery will take place. But this is the overture. It must offer contrast, and so Strauss pulls it back, to a *piano* repeat of the opening. Mustn't give too much of the plot away yet.

And back comes the great opening waltz, again that stroke of genius to have it played *pianissimo*, make the audience strain forward to be sure they can catch it. Then give it to them full, *forte*.

The second waltz returns, now *fortissimo*, with high leaps once again in the first violins. Back comes the march, *piano*, then strings and wind in unison as the pace quickens. Notes fly off into the air, *fortissimo* now, and a sequence of unison chords tells us the overture is about to reach its climax – and end.

Eight chords – chord, pause, chord, pause, chord, pause ... – the audience cannot help but hold its breath. The final three chords sound – two swift chords and an end chord. Syncopated. Unexpected. And the applause and cheers break out.

I have seen composers turn to the audience, having conducted one of their own works. They are not of this planet, not of our world. Johann Strauss at this moment must have resembled the Lenbach portrait, eyes blazing, staring before him and seeing nothing. His forehead will have been glistening with sweat, his clothes damp.

Is it too much to surmise that the audience rose to its feet, refused to let him head straight for the exit, shaking his hand, clapping him on the shoulders as he struggled to leave, the curtain already back, Rosalinde on stage, her admirer Alfred off stage and waiting for the cue to begin his opening number?

He should, of course, have retired to his personal box, reclined in a comfortable easy chair, and enjoyed the performance of his masterpiece. Instead he had ordered a carriage to be ready to take him back to his house on the Igelgasse, and Adèle.

He emerged into the light of a spring afternoon. The air tasted good, permeated with the scent of lilac and acacia. Horse-chestnut trees in full white blossom lined the streets. But there was still a hint of a lingering late-winter chill, and so Johann turned the collar of his coat up, wincing slightly at the touch of cold sweat on his skin.

He needed to walk, breathe freely. He dismissed the carriage with a wave of the hand and began the walk back to his house. It was by no means a short stroll. Johann knew it would take a half-hour or more, along the Ringstrasse and then south into the district of Wieden.

Did he regret the decision after ten or fifteen minutes, as his body warmed from the exertion, but the sweat stayed clammy on his forehead and neck? Did he stop and sit on a bench and dab his face with a handkerchief? We know that by the time he entered his own front door his face had lost its colour, his skin was cold and clammy, and he was finding it an effort to breathe normally.

Adèle ordered him straight to bed to rest. But he was soon back at his stand-up desk working on *Aschenbrödel*. The fever, though, would not pass, and Adèle made him wear warmer and warmer clothes. She summoned the family doctor, Dr Lederer, who examined Johann and told Adèle he needed to call in a specialist.

Professor Dr Hermann Nothnagel of the University of Vienna was summoned. He placed a stethoscope against Johann's back and asked him to cough.

Johann did as he was told, then asked, 'Is that all I can do for medical science?'

Five days after conducting the overture to *Die Fleder-maus*, on Saturday, 27 May, he began to suffer severe shivering fits and vomiting. He had a high fever. Dr Nothnagel, aware of Johann's phobia of anything to do with illness or death, told him he had a severe cold. He told Adèle her husband had double pneumonia.

Johann was confined to his bed. On 1 June he began to lose consciousness and he became delirious. Adèle re-called later that in one of his lucid moments Johann, smiling weakly, sang a song in a feeble voice. It was a Viennese clas-sic, which she said even her young daughter knew. She also knew that it was written by the composer Joseph Drechsler, who had taught Johann as a young man, but she had never heard him sing it before. It had a gently turning melody and the words were particularly apt:

> *Brüderlein fein, Brüderlein fein*
> *Musst mir ja nicht böse sein,*
> *Scheint die Sonne noch so schön*
> *Einmal muss sie untergehn.*

> (Little brother, little brother so fine,
> Don't be cross, you'll forever be mine.
> Yet no matter how beautiful the sun does get
> Sooner or later it has to set.)

On the morning of Saturday, 3 June, Dr Nothnagel issued a bulletin:

*The inflammation has reached its peak, and has at-
tacked both lobes of the lungs in their entirety. The
fever is very high; the patient is unconscious.*

Later that morning Johann reached for his wife's hand and
kissed it twice without words.

'It was his last caress,' Adèle reported, 'at a quarter past
four he died in my arms.'

Johann Strauss the Younger, the best-loved composer
the city of Vienna had ever produced, died at the age of
seventy-three, six months short of a new year and a new
century.

On the same afternoon a concert was taking place in the
Vienna Volksgarten in aid of the memorial fund set up
to remember Johann Strauss senior and his one-time colleague, then rival, Joseph Lanner. The conductor was the
well-known composer, arranger, and collector of traditional Viennese songs, Eduard Kremser.

Every seat was taken, and concertgoers lined the pe-
rimeter of the park, enjoying family outings, drinks and
picnics, swaying to the traditional sounds of their city and
the Austrian countryside.

As one piece ended, someone went up to the podium,
tapped Kremser on the shoulder, and whispered in his ear.
For a moment Kremser stood quite still. Then he leant

towards the orchestra leader and said something to him. The first violinist passed the word to the desk behind, and it spread in whispers through the orchestra.

On every music stand a piece of sheet music was pulled out from behind and placed in the front. The string players put mutes on their instruments. Kremser raised his arms. The left arm was outstretched, palm down to indicate *pianissimo*. The right arm gave the most gentle of downbeats.

First and second violins sounded the shimmering open-ing chord, and in the next bar a solo French horn sounded the three rising quavers to a sustained note, woodwind re-sponding with light quavers. The beautiful melodies of *'By the Beautiful Blue Danube'* wafted on the summer air across the Volksgarten.

Thus Vienna learned of the death of its Waltz King.

Into the 1970s and 1980s those Viennese who remem-bered it as children still spoke of Johann Strauss's funeral as *eine schöne Leich* (a good funeral). Three days after his death, on the afternoon of 6 June, eight black horses drew a hearse bearing Johann's coffin, driven by men dressed in Renaissance Spanish costume, away from the house on the Igelgasse.

Six pallbearers drawn from the Society of the Friends of Music and the Vienna Authors' and Journalists'

Association 'Concordia' walked alongside, each bearing a red satin cushion.* On one was Johann Strauss's baton, on another a lyre, three bore his many medals, and on the sixth lay his violin with its strings sprung to signify that it would never be played again.

More dignitaries walked behind carrying flags and torches. A succession of carriages followed, overflowing with flowers and wreaths, and containing Adèle and close friends, Conservatory professors, artists, more than forty representatives of parliament and the city council, Vienna's mayor, Karl Lueger, and Gustav Mahler.

The cortège made its way past the Theater an der Wien to the Protestant Church in the Dorotheergasse, in recognition of Johann's 'conversion' to Lutheran Protestantism, part of the process that had enabled him to marry Adèle.

After the consecration service, the procession made its way past the Vienna Court Opera building and elaborate Musikverein concert hall, and then began the lengthy journey south-east towards the city boundary and the main cemetery, the Zentralfriedhof. Crowds lined the route, with many following on foot for the whole distance.

At the cemetery funeral orations were delivered by the Mayor of Vienna and representatives from the Vienna Musicians' and 'Concordia' Associations. Johann Strauss was buried in the Musicians' Quarter of the Zentralfriedhof,

---

* *Gesellschaft der Musikfreunde and Journalisten- und Schriftstellerverein 'Concordia'*

alongside his friend Johannes Brahms, and only yards from Beethoven and Schubert.

In the days that followed, eulogy after eulogy was printed, and the single factor that united them all was the recognition that the music of Johann Strauss *was* Vienna.

Guido Adler, Austrian composer and musicologist, devoted an entire music history lecture at the University of Vienna to Johann Strauss, saying:

> *Strauss's melodies strengthen the feeling of home for Viennese, for Austrians. One could say, 'Vienna lives in his sounds.' They are the musical reflection of the Viennese soul.*

The *Illustriertes Wiener Extrablatt* reported:

> *Now that he is dead, this great, kind Viennese master, it is as if one of the old, world-famous landmarks of Alt Wien has disappeared from the face of the city, demolished by death. Johann Strauss belongs to Vienna like the Prater or St Stephen's.*

And in the *Fremdenblatt*, these words:

> *In all parts of the world, on all seas, the name Johann Strauss was like our flag … We bury more than a composer. A proud piece of our fatherland is laid to rest.*

For days and weeks afterwards, hundreds then thousands of picture postcards featuring a variety of portraits of Johann Strauss went on sale, and remain so to this day.

What I find particularly striking is the extent to which the character of Johann Strauss instantly became identified with his music, and has continued to be so. He is universally portrayed, in image and words, as kindly, carefree and happy – just like his music. I wonder what Adèle, and those collaborators who felt the sharp edge of his tongue, would have to say to that.

Perhaps the most fulsome tribute to the Waltz King came three years before his death, from one Oskar Blumenthal, director of Berlin's Lessing-Theater. It is a perfect example of the character of the composer being subsumed in his music. Clearly, as I have shown, Johann Strauss was *not* the carefree soul that his music would suggest. Yet so strong is the legend that I still find it hard to argue with any aspect of this assessment:

> *For fifty years Johann Strauss has, although unseen, been present at almost every joyous function of the civilised world. Wherever parties of happy people have gathered for carefree pleasure, Johann Strauss's spirit has pervaded. If we could estimate the amount of happiness and enjoyment contributed to the world by his creations, Johann Strauss would be regarded as one of the greatest benefactors of the century.*

Some years ago I interviewed the president and first violinist of the Vienna Philharmonic Orchestra, Dr Clemens Hellsberg, for a radio programme I was making entitled *Vienna, City of Music.*

We stood in the aisle of the Golden Hall of the Musikverein, gilded statues looking down on us. Dr Hellsberg pointed to the spot above the stage on the left where Johannes Brahms sat and heard a performance of his Fourth Symphony, just a month before he died.

We spoke of Bruckner and Wagner, Mahler and Richard Strauss. Finally I asked him a question I was determined to ask, but hesitated to do so in case he dismissed it with a wave of the hand, as if to say, 'We are talking of *serious* music here.'

I asked, 'Here we are in Vienna, in the famous concert hall where the New Year's Day concert takes place every year, and where the *"Blue Danube Waltz"* is heard each time. What is it about the music of Johann Strauss, do you think, that makes it so enduring and so universally loved?'

A smile instantly settled on his face, much to my relief. He thought for just a brief moment, and then said, 'Strauss makes you happy.'

There was one notable absentee from Johann Strauss's funeral: his brother Eduard. Life had not been kind to the youngest of the Strauss brothers. He was now sixty-four and a man with problems.

He was also a man with a plan. It was an extraordinary plan, to us an inexplicable one. He would soon commit the single worst act of vandalism in the history of music.

Chapter 20

Eduard's Flames of Revenge

As we have seen, Eduard and his elder brother had never really got on. In the way that siblings often do, they agreed about little and there was coolness – even animosity – between them. It was long-lasting. As late as 1892, when Johann was sixty-six and Eduard fifty-seven, Johann wrote to his publisher, 'Brother Eduard is not the sort who is inclined to want to say something that pleases me.'

It is difficult to assess now who was more to blame. There are contradictory comments about each man's behaviour. Eduard's eldest son Johann certainly followed his uncle Josef in initially putting his natural musical talent to one side and pursuing an entirely different career. In his case it was to study law at the University of Vienna, and then take up a post as an accounts official in the Ministry of Education and Instruction.

But, as he himself said, paying tribute to his other famous uncle:

I had music in my blood, and I longed to get away from the tedium of the public functionary. It was my paternal uncle, Johann, who especially understood that I had a talent for music. He supervised my efforts as a composer, he even allowed me to transcribe his own orchestral compositions for piano, and he encouraged my musical studies in every way.

Eduard, his father, was having none of this. He said, 'My brother never bothered about the upbringing or education of my sons.'

Which is the accurate account? We cannot know for sure. What is certain is that Eduard had every reason to be bitter. Remember Johann refusing to adjust his will when he heard that Eduard had encountered financial difficulties? This came about through an appalling set of circumstances that afflicted Eduard, and which must have devastated him utterly.

It is highly arguable that Eduard was the hardest-working member of the Strauss family. His compositions, like those of his father and two brothers, run into the hundreds, even if they are not as memorable or enduring as most of theirs. And when it comes to orchestral touring and management he was in a league of his own.

In the single year of 1890 he made a triumphant tour

throughout the United States and Canada, lasting twenty-nine weeks, and performed in sixty-two American towns and cities – that's an average of one concert every three days for seven months – and over the following nine years he made concert tours to Germany, Russia, the Netherlands and England, as well as performing in his home city of Vienna.

This amassed Eduard a considerable fortune, but in 1897 he was suddenly confronted by the realisation that almost everything he'd earned had been squandered by his wife and two sons. In the three-year period from 1894 to 1897, Eduard's two sons, apparently with the knowledge and support of their mother, had spent a total of 738,600 kronen.[*]

Eduard was in despair at this turn of events. On tour in London, he poured his heart out to a friend in a letter dated 21 July 1897, which makes a clear if oblique reference to his elder brother's refusal to help:

> *I do not know if you have heard about the limitless distress which I suffer due to the profligacy of the members of my family, and the position and the circumstances force me to stand completely alone! I no longer have a family! Let me not dwell on this unspeakably sad situation any longer.*

---

[*] Around £1 million in today's money.

It seems difficult, if not impossible, for us today to know exactly how or why the money was squandered. I have been unable to unearth any details; it is quite possible Eduard never revealed what was behind it, or even destroyed the evidence. All we know is that after he discovered the loss, Eduard went to his elder brother for financial help, and was refused.

The affair ended Eduard's marriage. He separated from his wife Maria, and became largely estranged from his two sons.

All of which meant that if Eduard was dreaming of a comfortable retirement, he needed to think again. In the autumn of 1899, at the age of sixty-four, and just months after the death of Johann (by which time we can assume he knew from Johann's will that he was to receive nothing), he signed a contract for yet another intensive tour.

He was off to North America again, almost a decade after the last tour. In a period of just under four months, spanning the turn of the century, he gave daily concerts and matinées twice a week, a total of 106 concerts, in seventy-three different places.

Now in his mid-sixties, Eduard paid the price for his exacting itinerary. In New Orleans, Chicago and San Francisco he had to be treated for malaria, while in Montreal it was problems of a different nature. The large French-speaking community was angry that advertisements for the concerts were placed only in the English-language newspapers, and so boycotted the concerts.

Troubles for Eduard and his orchestra did not end there. In the early morning of 7 February 1901, with just five engagements left, the train they were travelling on was involved in a collision as it pulled into Pittsburgh. Eduard dislocated his right shoulder.

For the remaining concerts, which culminated in a benefit ball in New York, Eduard was forced to conduct with his left arm, no doubt in considerable pain from the dislocation. At the end of the ball he knew he was laying down his baton for the last time. Did it make him sorrowful, or even nostalgic as he remembered the high points of an illustrious career? Not a bit of it. A letter he wrote made it clear he had firmly disliked every moment:

> *As I laid down my baton at the ball … I knew that I had now conducted for the last time, and I cannot describe what feelings came over me in this moment when, after thirty-nine years' work with all its unpleasantness, rancour, troubles, sorrows, deprivations and exertions … I had now reached my goal.*

Here was a man as far removed from the traditional image of the swaying Strauss, composer and performer of lovely melodies, as it is possible to be. If his elder brother did not conform to that traditional image, how much further removed from it was his younger brother!

If we take Eduard at his word (and all his writings and utterings seem to confirm it) he had not only been a reluctant musician, but he had not enjoyed any of it. It is possible to argue that to some extent he was responsible for this – he was a difficult man who resented living in his elder brother's shadow, and it was on his shoulders that the rigours, even tedium, of touring fell – but that does not alter the fact that he was not happy in his job.

It is not difficult, then, to envisage the pleasure with which he laid down his baton in New York, and the joy with which he summoned the forty-two players in the Johann Strauss Orchestra the following morning. They must have known what was coming.

At eleven o'clock on the morning of 13 February 1901 Eduard disbanded the Johann Strauss Orchestra, almost seventy-six years after his father founded it. He himself had managed it, and conducted it on tour, for the previous thirty years.

Did he do this with any sense of nostalgia, gratitude even for the players who had worked so hard for him? Was he grateful for their loyalty? Not exactly. These are the words he wrote: 'I was overjoyed to have nothing more to do with this category of men.' They must have wondered how they had come to upset him so much.

When Eduard returned to Vienna, he had earned enough from the tours to be able to retire, giving up all his public duties. He was sixty-five. In November he was awarded a medal for services to music. The invitation to the prestigious event named the recipient of the honour as *Johann* Strauss. You can just imagine Eduard's fury –

or maybe by this stage in his life it was a resigned shrug of the shoulders.

I mentioned Eduard had problems at home, of which his musicians must have had more than an inkling. It was public knowledge that Eduard separated from his wife after the scandal of the squandered money. They are certain to have known too that his son Johann had been investigated for possible bankruptcy. This happened again in 1901, and will have alienated father and son still further.

Johann's money problems might have been due to the fact that he had formed his own orchestra, with which he gave his first concert in Vienna on 3 November 1900, possibly deliberately timed to take place while his father was in the United States.

For a time he seemed to inherit the Strauss mantle by directing the music at the balls of the Imperial Court, still presided over by the old Emperor Franz Josef. But the coveted title of Court Ball Music Director, held both by his uncle and his father, eluded him, almost certainly because of his brushes with the law.

Financial problems continued for Johann, and matters came to a head when, on 5 October 1904, he stood in the dock accused of bankruptcy incurred through negligence, and defrauding his creditors. After painfully lengthy proceedings he was convicted, ordered to pay a large fine, and sentenced to a week's imprisonment.

Johann Strauss, bearer of such a famous name, nephew of the most famous musician the city of Vienna had produced, serving time in jail! It was an unthinkable path for a member of this most illustrious of musical families to have gone down.

If Eduard was estranged from his son before, this was the final straw. Unimaginable shame had been brought on the family. He wanted nothing more to do with either of his sons.

It was in this frame of mind, fully retired from the world of music, bitter, angry, resentful, that Eduard Strauss put into action an unthinkable act of vandalism. Is it too much to call it the ultimate act of revenge? You must judge for yourself, but I do not believe so.

We have two people's word only for what I am about to describe. The first is Eduard's, and refers to the reason behind the act. The second is the factory owner who carried it out under Eduard's orders.

In September 1907 Eduard made enquiries of oven manufacturers and incinerator plants in Vienna. He wanted to know if they would incinerate 'several hundred kilos of waste paper', which he had accumulated and wanted to get rid of.

He finally settled on one in the Mariahilf district of the city and agreed on a price of two kronen per hundred kilos. On 22 October 1907 a furniture van crammed full of tied bundles of waste paper arrived at the plant.

A small team of men unloaded the van and began to untie the bundles. The factory owner gave the paper a cursory glance, then looked more closely and realised that it was manuscript paper, covered in staves and musical notes. He knew he was looking at compositions by the famous Strauss family.

He had all the bundles untied, until the floor was deep in manuscript paper: hundreds, possibly thousands, of pages, all covered in notes. He decided to wait until Eduard Strauss himself arrived, which he was due to do at around two o'clock.

When Eduard arrived the factory owner tried to make light of the matter, suggesting to Eduard that there was possibly some mistake, since this was obviously not waste paper but something altogether more worthwhile and valuable.

To his surprise Eduard assured him that this was indeed the waste paper he wanted incinerated. The factory owner tried to dissuade Eduard, telling him his men would happily bundle it all up again and deliver it back to his address.

Eduard was adamant. He repeated he wanted to see every sheet go up in flames. The factory owner gave the order. Eduard Strauss sat in an armchair in front of two large kilns for firing pottery, and watched as the men fed the sheets of paper into the flames.

Occasionally, the proprietor recalled, Eduard was visibly moved when he saw particular sheets of music that held special memories. Every so often he would look away, or stand up, or walk into the office to gather himself. But not once did he ask for a sheet of music to be spared from the flames.

Eduard stayed until the very end, until the last sheet of paper had been burned – all the more remarkable, the factory owner reported, since there was so much paper it took fully five hours for it all to be fed to the flames, the final sheet not being consumed until seven o'clock in the evening. Only then did Eduard, satisfied, leave the premises.

Later it was learned that as if this was not enough, Eduard took two further vehicle-loads full of completed manuscript paper to another factory in the Porzellan-gasse, and had them all destroyed too.

What had occasioned this extraordinary act? We have only Eduard's word for it, as he described it in the memoirs he wrote in retirement, and even then he makes only passing reference to it.

He recounts that way back in 1869 he entered into a 'social contract' with his brother Josef, who was already suffering from the headaches and occasional fainting fits that would kill him a year later.

Josef feared that his life was in danger and, according to Eduard, agreed to make over all performing rights in his music to Eduard, in return for which Eduard would make financial provision for Josef's widow and daughter.

More than that, again according to Eduard, the brothers agreed that if Josef should die and Eduard was subsequently to give up his musical activities, then Eduard should destroy all Josef's papers, as well as providing in his will for the destruction of his own papers.

The motive, Eduard explained, was to prevent valuable material penned by a Strauss from falling into the hands of unscrupulous persons who might pass off the works as their own.

Can we believe Eduard's account? The most that can be said is that it is the only explanation we have of this extraordinary act. It is a fact that in the year before he died Josef himself said he was turning to other kinds of composition. The *Morgenpost*, in its obituary of him, said he died before he could realise 'the most precious ambition of his life – the composition of a grand opera'.

Josef's widow and daughter both claimed in writing that Josef was working on an operetta. If either the *Morgenpost* or his wife and daughter – possibly both – were correct, then all we know for sure is that such a work disappeared, never to be found.

Is it unreasonable to suggest that Eduard, to avoid unfavourable comparisons with his brother, found the work and destroyed it after Josef's death? In light of what was to happen more than thirty years later, perhaps not.

On that grim day at the incinerator plant, and the other even more destructive day at the second plant, we can assume that several hundred, quite possibly several thousand, compositions went up in smoke. We have an eyewitness account of bundles of paper being shovelled into the two kilns at the first plant, and that it took a full five hours. Add to that two vehicle-loads at another plant.

That is a lot of material, and it has to be more than Josef alone could have produced. Another account[*] has Eduard's chin quivering with emotion as he recognised his father's or Josef's writing on some of the sheets of paper. This suggests letters, articles, quite possibly librettos as well as compositions – all went up in smoke.

It is beyond doubt that the enormous amount of papers included compositions, as well as letters and other documents, by Johann Strauss himself, as well as his father and brother Josef. Eduard himself catalogued them before destroying them, making his actions all the more extraordinary. Who knows what great compositions, as well as valuable material relating to this most prodigious of musical families, might have been lost in those few dire days of 1907?

Eduard Strauss lived on, alone, for nine more years, in increasingly declining health. He saw the music of the Strauss family slowly fall out of favour, as names such as

---

[*] In Heinrich Eduard Jacob, *Johann Strauss: Father and Son – A Century of Light Music* (The Greystone Press, 1940).

Franz Lehár, Oskar Straus and John Philip Sousa competed for public attention.

Eduard Strauss suffered a fatal heart attack on the night of 28 December 1916, and died in the presence of his housekeeper. He was eighty-one years of age. His death brought to an end a golden epoch of Viennese music-making, and closed two generations in the most prolific and popular musical family, not just in Vienna but in musical history.

Chapter 21

A New Century and a New Vienna

In some ways it is just as well that Johann Strauss died in the final year of the nineteenth century. He was every inch a man of that century. He was born just four years after Napoleon died, two years before Beethoven died, into a country that was still predominantly agricultural and a city that had not yet felt the effects of the industrial revolution that was to transform Europe. The Vienna in which he died seventy-three years later was a bustling city echoing to the new sounds of the motor and mechanisation. One can almost imagine him covering his ears in horror as the first electrical tramline began to clatter over the cobbles in 1897.

He had witnessed the city of his birth transform itself from a small inner city hemmed in – literally – by a massive ring of fortifications, with a mere quarter of a million souls living both inside the wall and in the villages close by outside it, into a modern metropolis of nearly one and a half million people jostling for living space.

By the end of the century much had changed, but in another sense it had stayed the same. The immigrants who had thronged the streets of the inner city dressed in colourful traditional clothes were now the underclass of the suburbs, engaged in menial tasks and dressed shabbily. But they were still there, guarding their nationalist traditions. Vienna was still the crossroads of Europe, and therefore still the musical capital of Europe.

Small wonder the music of the Strauss family found a ready audience. Native Viennese recognised its essentially Germanic – and therefore Austrian – quality. The waltz, after all, had its beginnings in the stomping *Ländler* of the Black Forest. The two countries shared a language, and much else, and great German musical names such as Brahms and Schumann (to name but two) found as ready an audience in Vienna as in their home towns.

Those of other ethnic origins were naturally drawn to the music of the Strausses as they assimilated, along with their own traditions, the traditions of the country to which their parents, or grandparents, had emigrated.

Throughout the century other composers, other musicians, had come and gone, but Vienna's Johann Strauss had stayed in his home city. 'One of us,' his admiring fellow Viennese would say.

Fitting, then, that in the final decade and a half, or slightly more, of the century, of the many great musical names to take their final bow, Johann Strauss was the only Viennese and also the last to leave. Wagner had died in 1883, Liszt three years later. Tchaikovsky, who visited Vienna many times and described it as the city he 'liked almost more than any city in the world', died in 1893. Anton Rubinstein and Hans von Bülow died in 1894, Franz von Suppé in 1895, and Anton Bruckner one year later. Strauss was profoundly affected when his old friend Johannes Brahms passed away in 1897, preceding him by two years.

The four-year period between von Suppé dying in 1895 and Johann Strauss four years later, the Viennese referred to as *das grosses Sterben* ('the great dying'). What has come to be known as 'The Golden Age' was over, and it ended definitively with the death of Strauss.

The one important musical name to carry the torch into the new century was Gustav Mahler, resident of Vienna but again not Viennese. Mahler was a friend of the artist Gustav Klimt and found himself closely involved in what came to be known as the Viennese Secession, a movement across the arts determined to break away from the old traditions. It took hold as the old century gave way to the new. If the primary aim of those involved was to shock, the results were none the worse for that. Works of art – paintings, sculptures, architecture, music, literature – were created that today are considered to be masterpieces.

The close links between music and the Secession are exemplified in the Secessionist Building, an exhibition hall topped by its famous 'golden cabbage' cupola, which contains Klimt's *Beethoven Frieze*. This extraordinary work of art extends 110 feet across four walls.* Both building and frieze stand today as testament to the creativity of the Viennese Secession.

If the *fin de siècle* was a time of dying in Vienna, it was also a period of rebirth – more *début de siècle* than *fin* in some ways. Artists of all kinds were taking their art in entirely new directions. In 1897 Gustav Klimt caused a sensation in Vienna when he led a band of nineteen like-minded artists out of the Imperial Academy to form their own modernistic movement.

Egon Schiele was later to cause a sensation of a different kind with nude paintings of such graphic detail – including paintings of his sister – that he landed himself in prison for exhibiting erotic drawings where they could be seen by children.

Sigmund Freud published his ground-breaking work *The Interpretation of Dreams* in 1899, introducing an entirely new way of approaching mental problems – psychoanalysis – to an unsuspecting world.

In literature Arthur Schnitzler, a qualified doctor, confronted the anti-Semitism rabid in Viennese society head

---

* A musicians' 'Walk of Fame', or 'Music Mile', runs past the Secessionist Building and Opera House on its way from the Theater an der Wien to St Stephen's Cathedral – paving stones bearing the names of great musicians associated with Vienna (in overt imitation of the Hollywood Walk of Fame).

on, in a way that no one had dared to do before. That was not the only way in which he shocked. One of his plays depicted a circular chain of ten pairs of characters before and after having sex, beginning and ending with the same prostitute. Vienna had literally never seen anything like it. Schnitzler was dismissed in refined quarters as a pornographer.

In architecture too there was a wilful break with the past, led by Adolf Loos (even if he attacked the Secessionists rather than joined them). He considered any kind of ornamentation to be superfluous, and designed stripped-down buildings – an early precursor of the minimalist movement.

His most famous, i.e. notorious, building was commissioned in 1909 and constructed directly opposite the Hofburg Palace on the Michaelerplatz. The six-storey building has pillars on the front, with four floors above. Most of the windows have windowboxes below them, but none has any ornamentation above it. The Viennese called it 'the building without eyebrows'.

Emperor Franz Josef could clearly see the building from his palace, and utterly loathed it. After it was built he never again used the palace exit on to the Michaelerplatz, so he did not have to set eyes on it. He even had the windows that gave out on to the Michaelerplatz nailed shut, so he would not inadvertently catch a glimpse of it.*

---

* The Looshaus, as it is now known, was damaged by bombs in 1944 and put under protection in 1947. It was elaborately renovated in 1987 and looks today very much as it did when it so offended the emperor's eyes.

If so much had changed, then, there was one constant in Vienna, in Austria, in the Austro-Hungarian empire, that had not changed one jot, and showed no sign of doing so. It was an old man who wished he could die.

At the turn of the century Emperor Franz Josef was seventy years of age. He was already one of the longest-reigning monarchs in European history,[*] and if his accession to the throne was – literally – a lifetime ago, it must also have seemed to belong to another world.

Like Johann Strauss, Franz Josef was moulded by the nineteenth century. Here was a man who had suffered untold personal tragedy, seeing the world slip away from him into a new era. He must have longed to retire, to live peacefully in Bad Ischl with Kathi Schratt.

Instead he ruled over a fractious and diverse empire, extending from Innsbrück in the west to beyond the Carpathians towards the Black Sea in the east, a vast area of central Europe containing no fewer than ten independent states, one of which – Serbia – was shortly to play a tragic role in world history.

Franz Josef truly was now *'der alte Herr'*, the 'Old Gentleman' beloved of his people. He knew his time was past,

---

[*] France's Louis XIV reigned for longer, and although Queen Victoria had been on the throne longer at the turn of the century, she would die the following year.

and his people knew it too. As the first decade of the new century progressed, a saying took hold in Vienna: 'It will be the end of Austria when the Old Gentleman closes his eyes.' It was said always with affection and respect, though those who uttered it can have had no inkling of how appallingly prophetic the words were.

Nor can they have understood just what was occupying the emperor's mind. Only those truly close to him could have had any inkling. He lived in fear of becoming senile, incapacitated mentally and unable to rule. He had long since given up any hope of an easy natural death around his three score years and ten. It seemed he was destined – condemned – to live on and on. Perhaps the greatest tragedy of all those that afflicted him was that he simply could not die, and therefore was unable to find peace and release.

Franz Josef had always done his duty but he was finding it harder and harder to master any political brief, to the frustration of his ministers and generals. Increasingly they bypassed him, albeit subtly, making decisions, and at the same time positioning themselves to take full advantage of the power struggles that would follow the inevitable.

As the awful and portentous year of 1914 approached, an exhausted old man sat on the imperial throne in the Hofburg Palace, struggling to keep in touch with fast-moving political events.

Those events were about to spiral out of control and Franz Josef, in responding to them, would unwittingly take a course of action for which the description 'catastrophic' would prove to be absurdly weak.

After Crown Prince Rudolf's suicide at Mayerling back in 1889, the heir to the Habsburg throne was the emperor's nephew, Archduke Franz Ferdinand, a pompous and difficult man for whom Franz Josef had little affection. His personal servant wrote in his memoirs that when the emperor and Franz Ferdinand were in the room together, 'thunder and lightning always raged as they had their discussions'.

In a grim and infinitely more portentous echo of the assassination of Empress Sisi more than a decade earlier, in June 1914 a group of Serb nationalists slipped into Sarajevo with orders to assassinate Archduke Franz Ferdinand. The ultimate aim of the conspiracy was to break off parts of Serbia from the Austro-Hungarian empire, as part of a wider ambition to restore Serbia to the broader frontiers and greater power it enjoyed in centuries past.

A bizarre, almost unbelievably absurd sequence of events led to a successful assassination. At first they botched it. A bomb thrown at the archduke's car bounced off the hood, exploded under the next car and wounded two officers. But Franz Ferdinand was unharmed and, accompanied by his wife, continued to a morning engagement at the Town Hall.

With typical brashness he interrupted the mayor's speech of welcome with the words: 'Mr Mayor, I came here on a visit and I get bombs thrown at me. It is outrageous.' Only after his wife calmed him down did he allow the mayor to continue with his speech.

The engagement over, the archduke instructed his driver to take him and his wife to the local hospital to visit those who had been injured in the bomb attack. In a single innocent error, which would echo down the years, the driver took a wrong turning and found himself back in the street where the bomb had been thrown, ironically named Franz Josef Strasse.

As it happened, one of the would-be assassins, the Bosnian-Serb Gavrilo Princip, was standing outside a café in the same street, no doubt bemoaning the failure of the mission. He instantly spotted the archduke's limousine, and must have watched bemused as the driver, realising his mistake, put his foot on the brake, slammed the gear lever into reverse, and tried to back out.

But the gears locked and the engine of the car stalled. It gave Princip exactly the opportunity he needed to carry out the task that had brought him to Sarajevo. He calmly walked towards the stationary car and fired two shots at his – literally – sitting targets.

The archduke's wife Sophie, hit in the abdomen, instinctively covered her husband's body with her own. Franz Ferdinand, bleeding from a wound in the neck, cried out to his wife, 'Sophie darling! Sophie darling! Don't die! Stay alive for our children!' (*'Sopherl! Sopherl! Sterbe nicht! Bleibe am Leben für unsere Kinder!'*)

By the time the limousine arrived at the hospital, both the archduke and his wife were dead, and the history of the world was about to change.

Back in Vienna the old emperor, eighty-three years of age, was once again brought news of the sudden and violent death of a member of his family. Old and frail in mind and body maybe, but he immediately realised the import of what had happened.

First and foremost the heir to the Habsburg throne was dead, the second to die suddenly. What would this mean for the dynasty? On a broader front it was almost inevitable that once Austria issued any kind of ultimatum against Serbia in response, Russia would come to the support of the Serbs, threatening the empire. This meant that Austria had to mobilise, to protect itself. At least that was what the emperor's ministers persuaded him was beyond question.

But wait, he said, further advice was needed, and he sought it from a ruler who was younger, more in tune with events, with a larger and more efficient army, than him. Kaiser Wilhelm, Emperor of Germany.

The kaiser's response was instant and reassuring. In the event of war with Russia, Germany would enter hostilities on the side of Austria. It was exactly the reassurance Franz Josef sought, but he was under no illusions.

'Now we can no longer turn back. It will be a terrible

war,' he said. That judgement was wrong only in the sense of it proving to be a gross understatement.

And what were the people of Vienna doing in the years leading up to these momentous events? They were doing what they had been doing for decades, doing what came naturally and enjoying the gaiety and laughter that ran in their blood. This was the city that had invented *Gemütlichkeit*.

It is the ability to understand that the key to happiness is the acceptance of what one cannot change. It is the message of *Die Fledermaus*, the single masterwork by Johann Strauss that so perfectly captured the mood of the Viennese and encapsulated it in music.

And so the Viennese were continuing to waltz, to escape into the essentially Viennese world of operetta. Johann Strauss was with them no more, they had lost their Waltz King, but there was another name now receiving their praise and adulation.

This time it was a composer born many miles from Vienna, and even in another country, who settled in Vienna, composed his music there, and became in all but name a Viennese. Franz Lehár might never have earned the sobriquet 'The Waltz King', and his world was more that of operetta than the pure waltz, but he could turn out a composition to stand comparison with those of any of the Strausses.

In 1902 the Viennese thrilled to his *'Gold and Silver Waltz'*, composed for the Gold and Silver Ball of a member of the aristocracy, and only three years later he produced an operetta whose success came closer to that of *Die Fledermaus* than anything else either he or Johann Strauss wrote: *Die Lustige Witwe*, 'The Merry Widow'.

The era of Johann Strauss was ended; but there were new names and new forms of entertainment on offer. The dance hall had given way to the café, the waltz had yielded to the operetta.

A new generation of Viennese was enjoying life just as their parents and grandparents had before them. They had the same emperor but in other ways they had broken with the past. It was a new century in a multitude of different ways.

Music, though, was still in their blood. It coursed through their veins as it had done for centuries past. The Viennese would still sing and dance, but now it would be to the music of a new generation of composers. And they would, of course, drink champagne for years and years to come. There was, surely, nothing that could take these pleasures away.

And then Gavrilo Princip fired those shots.

Chapter 22

The Nazis Rewrite History

During the first half of the twentieth century, the Habsburg empire consigned to history, Franz Josef long dead, having finally been granted his wish at the age of eighty-six, the defeated German kaiser dethroned and in exile in the Netherlands, Europe continued to reverberate to the music of Johann Strauss.

Johann III recovered from his financial woes, put his brief prison sentence behind him, and began to benefit from new technology to make the first wax-cylinder recordings of his uncle's music with his 'Johann Strauss's Vienna Orchestra'.

He toured too. In 1931, taking full advantage of sharing the name of the great composer, he subtly renamed the orchestra and performed at the Royal Albert Hall in London as 'Johann Strauss and his own Viennese orchestra'.

Johann Strauss III produced around thirty compositions, none of them coming close to anything his uncles or father had created. He died suddenly on 9 January 1939 at the age of seventy-two.

Perhaps he was fortunate to die just before the outbreak of the Second World War, for what would happen to the reputation of his family under the Nazis would surely have left him stunned and angry.

For the Nazis, keen to claim great German artists as the Aryan ideal – Richard Wagner being the prime example – Johann Strauss the Younger was an obvious candidate. His music was universally popular.

In June 1939 the Nazi newspaper *Der Stürmer* carried this description of him:

> *The whole world knows Johann Strauss, the Waltz King, with his incomparable melodies. There is hardly any other type of music which is so German and so close to the people as that of the great Waltz King. Johann Strauss is long since dead. He has become immortal.*

Hitler's Minister of Propaganda Joseph Goebbels lost no time in appropriating Strauss to the Nazi cause. But there were two inconveniences, one minor and one very major indeed.

The minor one was that Strauss was not actually German; he was Austrian.* This was solved in March 1938 when German troops marched into Vienna and Austria was annexed into the Third Reich, an event known as the *Anschluss*. Almost forty years after his death, Johann Strauss was now as German as someone born in Berlin.

The major problem for the man who in 1938 published 'Ten Principles of German Music Creativity', in which he explicitly called for all good Germans to fight against the infiltration of Jewish music in German culture, was that Johann Strauss had Jewish blood. Not very much – actually not quite enough to make him Jewish under the strict laws brought in by the Nazis themselves – but even a single drop was a drop too many.

It was there in writing for anyone to see. The register of St Stephen's Cathedral recorded the marriage of Johann's great-grandfather on 11 February 1762 thus:

> *Johann Michael Strauss, a respectable man, servant … a baptised Jew, single, born in Ofen, legitimate son of Wolf Strauss and his wife Theresia, both Jewish …*

According to the Nuremberg Laws of 1935, to be classified as German all four grandparents had to be Aryan. One or two grandparents only led to the classification of *Mischling*

---

* It seems either the Nazis did not know of his change of nationality to clear the path to his marriage, or discounted it.

('Half-caste'). Three grandparents who were Jewish, or a single parent (of either sex), meant you were Jewish.

Johann Strauss senior was therefore a *Mischling*, while his offspring were second-class *Mischlings*. This was not 'full-blooded' Jewishness by Nazi rules, and could even be upgraded to 'honorary Aryan' under certain circumstances, and with Hitler's personal approval.

But Goebbels did not want to go down that route. It was essential Johann Strauss the Younger was absolved of any Jewish connection. Goebbels recorded in his diary that Johann was one-eighth Jewish – in fact he was one-sixteenth – but that was one-eighth too much. He thus set in train one of the most bizarre acts of forgery perpetrated by the Third Reich.

The original register of St Stephen's Cathedral, recording great-grandfather Strauss's marriage, and his background, was removed and sent to the Department of Nationality and Race in Berlin, with orders from Goebbels that the offending entry should be carefully taken out, and then returned to Vienna.

One wonders how Goebbels or anyone found time to devote so much energy to the question of the Strauss family's Jewishness, given that they had a war to run, but devote it they did.

In Berlin the entire register was recorded page by page on microfilm, and a copy then produced on vellum, which was then bound in four volumes. Anyone examining the copy and looking for Johann Michael Strauss would find that he was missing. The next entry had been moved up to fill the gap. He had also been deleted from the index, so that the records no longer contained any evidence that the marriage had taken place.

The original, and copies, were returned to Vienna. The first page of volume one of the copies bore an official stamp of the Department of Nationality and Race, and the swastika seal of the Third Reich, certifying that it was an exact copy of the original. It was dated 20 February 1941.

That original, containing the entry for Johann Michael Strauss the Jew, was carefully hidden in the State Archive, well removed from St Stephen's Cathedral. The copies were replaced in the Cathedral.

There is a legend, impossible to verify, that in the spring of 1945, as the Nazis set about destroying Vienna as a farewell gesture, a man ran through the streets of the city clutching the original register. Determined to keep it safe, he secreted it in a deep vault beneath St Stephen's Cathedral. How he obtained it or who he was is unknown.

What is certain is that the original was found intact in that vault in the cathedral – not in the State Archive – after the war. It had survived the destruction of the city.

It was not until several years after the war that the whole bizarre episode came to light. On 8 June 1951 the Viennese newspaper *Arbeiter-Zeitung* published the story of the falsified document, explaining how the copies had been made and the entry for Johann Michael Strauss expunged.

If it is a blessing that the register survived, sadly not much else associated with Johann Strauss was so fortunate. Much of the inner city was destroyed in the Battle of Vienna, including the house in the Igelgasse, which Johann loved and where he so often sought sanctuary from the pressures on him.

What the Nazis did not destroy, the Soviet Red Army made short work of. Most of Johann's personal belongings, kept in various archives and museums, simply disappeared. Even his violin was gone.

For the Nazis, then, Johann Strauss was conveniently not Jewish, but two people he was extremely closely associated with most certainly were. His third wife Adèle was Jewish, a fact that had never been hidden, despite her conversion to Roman Catholicism in order to marry Strauss. This meant that her daughter Alice – Johann Strauss's stepdaughter – was Jewish too.

Adèle died in 1930 but Alice was in her early sixties at the outbreak of the Second World War. Johann, as I have related earlier, adored Adèle and doted on her young daughter. After his death a valuable part of his estate went to his widow, and from her to Alice.

The Nazi propaganda sheet *Der Stürmer* was having none of this. Johann's marriage to Adèle was an aberration, it claimed. He had been old and weak when he had met her,* and she had clearly taken advantage of him for her own gain.

It went further. With extraordinary perspicacity, not to say clairvoyance, it predicted exactly how Johann would have behaved had he lived half a century later under National Socialism, in a rant typical of Nazi propaganda:

> *If Johann Strauss were alive today, then he would be an anti-Semite. In his music lies true empathy for the* Volk. *Through his music a true German* [sic] *speaks to us. And precisely because we know this, we are therefore under an obligation not to let this great legacy be Jewified* (bejudeln lassen) *through Jewish eyes.*

It was a small and easy step to go from this to stating unequivocally that Alice had no right to inherit anything from her stepfather. Not only was Alice a Jew, the paper ranted, but she was falsifying information so that she could claim she was entitled to keep Strauss artefacts.

And even if she were entitled, what would she do then? Sell them to the highest bidder. Strauss himself had been aware of this danger, *Der Stürmer* reasoned in a wilful distortion of the facts, which was why he had donated his entire estate to Vienna's most prestigious and elite musical organisation, the *Gesellschaft der Musikfreunde*. It was nothing short of thievery that Alice was holding on to a

---

* He was in his mid-fifties.

large portion of it. She should donate it to the city of Vienna, the paper demanded.

Alice was worn down by a series of abusive articles in *Der Stürmer*. Now ageing and with no stomach for a fight, she saw herself robbed not only of the possessions and keepsakes her stepfather had given her, but of her dignity too.

Alice survived the Second World War and went to live in Switzerland. None of the possessions taken from her were ever returned, and she received no compensation. She died in 1945. It was not until the 1990s that it became known how the Nazis had treated her.

And what of the woman who all those years before had served Johann Strauss his favourite dish of crayfish and goose-liver pâté, washed down with dry champagne, and who had earned a place on the sideline of history as the emperor's closest companion for more than thirty years?

Katharina Schratt's world ended on 21 November 1916 when the Lord High Chamberlain telephoned her from Schönbrunn Palace to say that emperor was dead. Such was the life of a mistress.

Yet in an extraordinary acknowledgement of just how important she had been to the old man, and the esteem in which his family held her, courtiers at the palace had been given orders to admit her immediately into the private apartments, and then into the simple and austere bedroom where the emperor lay on the plain iron bed on which he had died.

The emperor's daughter, Archduchess Valerie, who had remained close to her father after Empress Sisi's tragic death, embraced her like a mother. Kathi walked to the bed, placed two white roses in the emperor's hands and bent over him, her eyes closed in prayer.

Franz Josef was buried with all the pomp of a great state funeral, sovereigns and princes of the empire converging on Vienna. But Kathi Schratt stayed away. She knew it was not her place to be there.

I expect that Kathi was in some ways grateful that the emperor did not live to see the end of the First World War, the defeat of Germany and Austria, and with it the abolition of the empire he had strived so hard to keep together.

Defeat brought financial hardship and ruin to the aristocratic classes and nobility. Money became worthless almost overnight, banks collapsed, the stock exchange crashed. Kathi was more fortunate than most, in that her assets were mainly in the form of gifts from the emperor and valuable artefacts she had collected over the years.

Soon a steady trickle of these made their way to the auction houses of Vienna, to keep Kathi afloat financially. On one occasion she asked her godson, who was attached to the Austrian Legation in London, to negotiate the sale of some valuable snuffboxes in the hope that Queen Mary might be interested. Apparently word came back from Buckingham Palace that the price was too high.

Those who might have expected Kathi to retire from public life, now that her usefulness at court was at an end, were to be disappointed. She reacquainted herself with her former world of the theatre, and many a young and impecunious actor found himself entertained at her table.

Sunday luncheons at her small house in Hietzing became famous in theatrical circles, with trays and confectionery sent round from Demel, the confectioner in the Kohlmarkt that was the city's best known.* There was a cacophony of sound, as boisterous conversation competed with the many stray dogs Kathi had collected and given sanctuary to.

Life in Vienna, once the most sophisticated city in Continental Europe, had changed for ever. Gone was the sumptuousness and grandeur of a capital city of empire, to be replaced by austerity and the shame of a defeated country.

None of this caused Kathi to retreat into obscurity. In her seventies she was still to be seen regularly at the Salzburg Festival, or taking a cure at the spa town of Karlsbad. In 1929, at the age of seventy-six, she boarded an aeroplane for the flight from Zurich to Vienna.

One thing Kathi Schratt did not do, though, which perhaps earns our admiration and frustration in equal measure. In the 1930s journalists beat a path to her door, offering large sums of money in foreign currencies for her memoirs – what we could call today a 'kiss-and-tell'.

---

* It still is.

All offers were politely but firmly refused, one such refusal reported and much admired. 'I was never a Pompadour, still less a Maintenon,' she said, in a witty and apt acknowledgement of her role.

Every now and then a sensational article would appear in a magazine, in which she was referred to as 'the emperor's sweetheart', or 'the *gnädige Frau* of Schönbrunn'. She told her friends she never read a word of any of them.

Only once did she react with anger at anything that was printed about her. She was furious when she was told one article said she had accepted a pension from Herr Hitler. She angrily denied it, and when later, in the spring of 1938, Hitler drove in triumph through Vienna after the *Anschluss*, she pulled down the blinds of her windows.

Kathi Schratt died on an April day in 1940. Like the man to whom she had devoted so much of her life, she was eighty-six years of age. Like him too, she died in the middle of a world war and did not live to see Austria defeated.

As for the innermost secrets of an emperor who had ruled for nearly seventy years, whose empire was no more, who had lost his brother, wife, son and nephew to assassination and suicide, whose shoulders bent – literally – under the intolerable weight of matters of state and personal tragedy, Kathi Schratt took them to her grave.

Chapter 23

Admired by the Greats

There was to be one more musical Strauss. Johann III's younger brother Josef, although a talented pianist, chose to become a garage proprietor, but Josef's youngest son Eduard – grandnephew of the Waltz King – decided on a musical career from the age of twelve.* He studied piano, horn and violin, took singing lessons, and made his conducting debut in 1949 – the centenary of the death of Johann Strauss the Elder, and fiftieth anniversary of the death of Johann Strauss the Younger.

Eduard II, as he was known, established a fine reputation as a conductor and was soon touring the world. In an extraordinary echo of his grandfather's limitless energy, in

---

* As I have noted, Eduard Strauss, younger brother of Johann and Josef, named his two sons after them. They in turn named each of their eldest sons after themselves!

1955 he conducted in Germany and Switzerland, and in the following twelve years he performed in Manila, Seoul, Moscow, Cairo, Paris, London, Athens, Gothenburg and Warsaw. During the same period he led six major tours of Japan, conducting no fewer than 137 concerts in 36 Japanese cities. It was an even more demanding schedule than his grandfather's, since he was also frequently in the recording studio.

In one respect only did he not inherit the Strauss genius. He was not a composer. He certainly tried, but told a friend, 'I was not at all satisfied that [my ideas] were of any value, and therefore threw them away.'

Eduard had firm ideas about how the music of his illustrious family should be played. The melodies, he said, should be allowed to unfold 'like a flower'. He was also adamant that the waltz should not be played too quickly: 'Always remember, people must be able to *dance* to it smoothly.'

Sadly Eduard died before reaching his sixtieth birthday (exhaustion, perhaps?), and with him the Strauss musical dynasty came to an end – four generations, six musicians, thousands of compositions, and a name synonymous with Vienna and the waltz.

Where, then, does the Strauss family stand in the lexicon of great musical names, and what is its legacy? I know what some might say. Strauss, the waltz, fluffy, light, easy on the ear, no depth, rather basic.

Well, think again. The catalogue of composers who admired Johann Strauss the Younger is long and illustrious, and these are not names anyone would regard as lightweight.

Hector Berlioz, who saw himself as the natural successor to Beethoven, said (as I noted earlier), 'Vienna without Strauss is like Austria without the Danube.'

I have already catalogued the friendship between Johann Strauss and Johannes Brahms, and the mutual respect that existed between them as composers. Remember, Brahms would have liked to have composed *'By the Beautiful Blue Danube'*, and recorded his wish in writing.

Tchaikovsky was an admirer, and expressed delight when he heard that one of his works, his *Characteristic Dances*, had been given its first public performance, conducted by Johann Strauss at one of his concerts in Pavlovsk.

Perhaps Johann Strauss's most ardent supporter – though I am not aware they ever met – is also the most unexpected. Second to none in his admiration for the Waltz King was a composer who never penned a frivolous note and to my knowledge never wrote a dance number, one Richard Wagner.

As a young man of nineteen, with no completed opera yet under his belt, Wagner came to Vienna and first heard Johann Strauss the Elder, later writing that vivid description of the concert that I have already quoted.

Wagner transferred his boundless admiration seamlessly from father to son. Thirty years later he called Johann Strauss the Younger 'the most musical brain of the age', and in a typically barbed comparison with other non-Germanic composers he could not have paid Johann a higher compliment:

> *A single Strauss waltz, as far as gracefulness, refinement and musical content is concerned, towers above the majority of the often laboriously procured foreign-produced creations.*

The admiration was entirely mutual. Johann Strauss frequently included orchestral passages from Wagner in his concerts and was incensed when, in 1861, the authorities at the Vienna Opera dropped plans to perform *Tristan und Isolde* because they considered it unplayable.

Johann wrote to Wagner asking for permission to play orchestral excerpts from the score. Wagner not only agreed but provided an orchestral version of the great *Love Duet* from Act II, and of Isolde's impassioned *Liebestod*.

In 1876, on his sixty-third birthday, after the most successful summer of his life, which had seen his custom-built theatre in Bayreuth finally open its doors, Wagner commanded – as was his wont – an orchestra to play for him under a popular local conductor.

His choice of music? The waltzes of Johann Strauss II. Relaxing in the front row of chairs alongside his wife

Cosima, relishing the ebb and flow of the music and its universally popular themes, suddenly he leapt up, seized the baton from the conductor's hands, and led the orchestra into the opening bars of *'Wein, Weib und Gesang'*.

Now there is a beguiling image. Richard Wagner, composer of the mightiest operas ever written, conducting a Strauss waltz!

I have already recounted how Gustav Mahler who, like Wagner, falls into the *über*-serious category, introduced *Die Fledermaus* to the Vienna Court Opera during Johann Strauss's jubilee celebrations. It has never left it, as the annual performance on New Year's Eve to this day testifies.

Yet another composer holds, as far as I know, the unique distinction of having taken a Strauss waltz and used it, deliberately not well disguised, in an opera of his own. He shared more than just the love of a waltz with the Strauss family; he shared a name too.

Richard Strauss was no relation to the Strauss dynasty. He was not even of the same nationality – German, rather than Austrian. But of his unbounded admiration for his namesake there can be no doubt.

He set his best-loved and most performed opera, *Der Rosenkavalier*, in the Vienna of Empress Maria Theresa, that golden age of the mid-eighteenth century when chivalry still ruled and Vienna rivalled Paris as the most dazzling capital city in Continental Europe.

At the end of Act II, after scenes of chaos and farce on stage, the pompous and much derided Baron Ochs, arm in a sling and drunk on copious quantities of port, dances around the stage ahead of what he believes will be an amorous tryst, unaware he has been thoroughly duped.

Richard Strauss writes a deliciously wry and ironic waltz and, given that this is Vienna, what better to base it on than one by one of his namesakes (never mind the anachronism that this Strauss lived a century *after* the action on stage)? He chose a well-known waltz by Josef Strauss, *'Dynamiden-Walzer'*.

Baron Ochs's waltz is not just similar to Josef Strauss's piece, the main theme is identical – a seductive leap of a sixth, followed by a fifth, and then a fourth. The only difference is a subtle variation in the length of the high notes.

No one can accuse Richard Strauss of plagiarism. He wanted the audience to recognise the work of a Strauss. How better to sum up the essence of Vienna? This is not supposition – he confirmed it himself. In an interview in the *Wiener Tagblatt* in 1925, he said (referring to Johann II), 'And with the waltzes from *Rosenkavalier* ... how should I not have thought of the laughing genius of Vienna?'

Finally, in the pantheon of unlikely musical admirers of Strauss, comes one of the most important British composers of the twentieth century, though one cannot help the feeling that Vaughan Williams was speaking rather begrudgingly when he said, 'A waltz of Johann Strauss is good music in its proper place.'

To say that the music of the Strausses lives on is something of an understatement. There is hardly a capital city in Europe, indeed in the developed world, that does not put on a concert of Strauss music to celebrate New Year.

The most famous of these is the New Year's Concert held in the gilded Musikverein in the city to which the Strauss family belonged, Vienna. The tradition began in the dark days of 1939 – the first such concert was actually held on New Year's Eve of that year, roughly a year and a half after Austria's annexation by Nazi Germany. In fact its origins were severely tainted. The concert was created for the purpose of appeasing and flattering the Nazi occupiers.

That was the first and last time the concert was held on New Year's Eve. There was a two-year hiatus caused by the war, then from 1941 it was held on New Year's Day – perhaps to signify a break with the past and its iniquitous origination – and has been every single year since.

Since 1987 it has become customary to invite a renowned maestro to conduct the concert, and some of the great names in conducting have performed the task – Herbert von Karajan, Carlos Kleiber, Lorin Maazel,[*] Claudio Abbado, Riccardo Muti, Daniel Barenboim, Zubin Mehta, to name but a few – but no one conducted more Vienna New Year concerts than Willi Boskovsky.

---

[*] On one occasion, Maazel put down his baton, lifted his violin, and played the zither solos at the start and end of 'Tales from the Vienna Woods'.

Not a conductor, but leader of the Vienna Philharmonic, Boskovsky believed in doing it the way the Strausses themselves did it, and he led the orchestra from the violin for twenty-five consecutive years. I have indelible images in my memory of watching the concert in black and white as a teenager in the 1950s and 1960s, Boskovsky swaying on the podium with his violin under his chin. It was the first time I had heard a Strauss waltz. I was transfixed, and remain so.

Traditionally the conductor conducts without scores, each piece committed to memory, and afterwards, applauded by admiring crowds braving the cold of a Viennese New Year's Day, he walks the red carpet from the Musikverein to the Hotel Imperial directly opposite for a celebratory glass of champagne.

Today the concert is beamed live around the world, and is watched by an audience of literally millions. So popular is it that if you wish to attend, your application has to be in by 31 January for the following year's concert, and then tickets are allocated by lottery. Some seats are held by Austrian families and are passed down from generation to generation.

The very first New Year's Concert consisted of music exclusively by Johann Strauss the Younger. Now it includes music by father and all three sons, as well as other composers – mainly Austrian – such as Lanner, Nicolai, von Suppé, even Mozart.

One thing is guaranteed. Two pieces will always be performed, although not in the programme itself but as encores. They are, quite simply, the two best-known compositions ever to come out of Vienna.

Surprising though it may seem, neither *'By the Beautiful Blue Danube'* nor the *'Radetzky March'* were performed in the early New Year's Concerts, and when they were included – *'Danube'* in 1945, *'Radetzky'* in 1946 – they were already encores. And that is how they have stayed.*

It is a firm tradition that after a number of lesser encores, the conductor cues the strings for the shimmering entry of the *'Blue Danube'*. He then stops them, turns to the audience, and he and the players shout *'Prosit Neujahr!'* ('Happy New Year') before beginning the piece again. After that he directs his baton to the percussionist for the side-drum roll that presages the *'Radetzky March'*.

I find it interesting, even ironic, that Johann Strauss the Younger's best-known and best-loved composition began life as a choral piece that flopped, and I wonder how many in the audience clapping and stamping their feet to the *'Radetzky March'* are aware that the *only* piece by Johann Strauss senior that remains firmly in the repertoire is the one that caused him to be booed off the podium in the wake of the 1848 revolutions.

---

* Two exceptions: in 1967 Boskovsky included *'By the Beautiful Blue Danube'* in the main body of the programme, and in 2004 Lorin Maazel left out the *'Radetzky March'* as a mark of respect for the victims of the Boxing Day tsunami.

Now imagine this. A young boy shows a natural aptitude for the violin, learns quickly, and by the time he is a teenager he has decided he wants a career as a musician. First, though, he has to convince an authoritarian father, a renowned musician himself, who is initially dismissive of the boy's musical talent and that of his brother too.

The boy achieves his ambition and becomes a professional musician. As a young man he decides to form his own orchestra, which he calls the Johann Strauss Orchestra. Instead of conducting, he leads from the violin.

The orchestra is small to begin with, just a dozen players, but it soon swells. Audiences flock to hear him, delighting in the seductive rhythm of the Viennese waltz and the lively beat of the polka.

Soon the orchestra leaves its home city and begins to tour Europe. Everywhere the players perform, ecstatic audiences applaud and dance, demanding encore after encore. Soon the Johann Strauss Orchestra is touring the world.

All true of Johann Strauss the Waltz King. True too of a certain André Rieu, born in 1949 in the Dutch town of Maastricht. Here the two names diverge, purely because of the advance of technology. André Rieu's albums have gone gold and platinum across the globe, and in his native Netherlands he is an eight-time platinum-selling artist.

In 2009 André Rieu was the world's most successful male touring artist, according to *Billboard* magazine. Of course this is due to the flair and showmanship of the

Dutchman, but it is also testament to the enduring popularity of the music of Johann Strauss.

Not so long ago I interviewed André Rieu for Classic FM. I asked him a question that had long been on my mind, I suppose from those early years watching the Vienna New Year's Day Concert on television. I wanted his answer to why I – and millions like me – find the music of Johann Strauss so instantly appealing and memorable, to the extent that as a boy of seventeen visiting Vienna, the only souvenir I brought home was an LP of Strauss waltzes.

'What is the answer, André? What is it about the music of Johann Strauss that beguiles and bewitches, that seduces the listener? What is the single quality that ensures its immortality?'

In a perfect echo of the interview I had conducted some years earlier with the president of the Vienna Philharmonic Orchestra, he thought for a moment – just a brief moment – then broke into a wide smile. 'Simple,' he said. 'Strauss makes you happy.'

I shall give the last word to the Waltz King himself, something he said to his wife Adèle, and on another occasion to a friend. He said it twice, so he must have meant it. This is the man who made Vienna, then Europe, then the world, dance to his music.

I am always being invited to dance, really tempting and attractive offers. But you know very well that I have never been able to dance, so every time my answer is a decisive 'no'.

Johann Strauss the Younger, the Waltz King, could not dance.

Afterword

I wrote this book for two reasons.

Vienna was the first place I ever went abroad without my parents. I was seventeen. It was a trip organised by the University of London (I can't remember how I found out about it). I had just started learning German at school, had never been so excited about learning anything in my short life, and pestered my dad until he allowed me to sign up.

I went to Vienna, and fell in love with the city and its music. Everywhere we went, the sounds of Strauss wafted on the air. I was entranced. (We went to a performance of Beethoven's *Fidelio* at the Vienna State Opera and I fell asleep.) On the final morning we were received by the mayor of Vienna in the great neo-Gothic Rathaus, and I was chosen to make a short speech of thanks in German. (It had been written for me, I stayed up the night before learning it so I would not have to read it, can still remember it word for word, and have been known to deliver it to anyone who upsets me enough.)

I knew nothing then about the dark side of the city, nor anything of the history of the Habsburg empire and its obliteration by the First World War. But my imagination was ignited, and remains brightly lit to this day.

That is the first reason. The second is that I do not believe such a book as mine exists, certainly not in the English language. Those that do are for the most part several decades old, and narrowly based.

Given the enduring popularity of the music of the Strauss dynasty, there are surprisingly few full biographies. In fact the word 'few' is itself an overstatement. Despite the full resources of the Internet, I have found just one.

It is *The Strauss Family*, by Peter Kemp (The Baton Press, 1989), part of the series *The Illustrated Lives of the Great Composers*, available now second-hand only on www. amazon.com for $0.96 and www.amazon.co.uk for £0.01.

I had the good fortune to meet Peter Kemp when I was asked to make the address at the annual dinner of the Johann Strauss Society of Great Britain in October 2003. He presented me with a copy of his book, which he told me ruefully had gone out of print soon after it was published in 1989. I knew at the time how lucky I was to have it in my possession.

It is an extraordinarily detailed book, interweaving the lives of the Strausses with their music, and I readily acknowledge my debt to it in writing my own book. What it does not do, though, is relate those lives to the city of Vienna and the turmoil of the Habsburg decline.

Nor do any other books on the Strausses that I have been able to find – in all cases they are deliberately narrow in scope.

The fullest account of their lives comes in *Johann Strauss: A Century of Light Music*, by Heinrich Eduard

Jacob (Hutchinson & Co., 1940). It is comprehensive, but again has little to offer on the turmoil of the nineteenth century and is inevitably dated.

The Viennese-born author Hans Fantel draws heavily on Jacob for his *The Waltz Kings: Johann Strauss, Father & Son, and The Romantic Age* (William Morrow & Co., 1972). This is good on the two Johanns, father and son, but has little on Josef and Eduard, and has more reflections from an American-based author longing nostalgically for his homeland than real history.

So we come to the more narrowly based books from the world of academia. The most recent is *The Legacy of Johann Strauss: Political Influence and Twentieth-Century Identity*, by Zoë Alexis Lang (Cambridge University Press, 2014). This is a doctoral study by Professor Lang of the Music Department of the University of Florida, and as its title suggests is more concerned with how Strauss was perceived in the twentieth century than in giving an account of his life. It is strong on the family's Jewish ancestry and the appropriation of the music by the Nazis – and their attempts to quash that Jewishness.

Johann Strauss: The End of an Era, by Egon Gartenberg (The Pennsylvania State University Press, 1974), is strong on the social history of Vienna, less so on the personal lives of the Strausses. The last third of the book concentrates on operetta in the twentieth century. I confess to having found it a dry read. Like the Kemp, it is available on Amazon second-hand only for cents or pennies.

Camille Crittenden was Associate Director of Institutional Gifts at San Francisco Opera when she wrote *Johann Strauss and Vienna: Operetta and the Politics of Popular Culture* (Cambridge University Press, 2006), as part of the Cambridge Studies in Opera series. She is, obviously, strong on the operettas and how they fitted in with the social life of Vienna, with barely a mention of the waltzes and polkas, and very little on the lives of the Strausses themselves.

When we come to the history of the Austro-Hungarian empire and the decline and fall of the House of Habsburg, there is a wealth of historical material with copious analysis of the reign of Emperor Franz Josef, though few try to get inside the mind of a man who lived through so many personal traumas. I have not found a single one with more than a passing reference to Johann Strauss the younger.

For a general history of Vienna, I have used *Vienna: Legend and Reality*, by Ilsa Barea (Secker & Warburg, 1966). Excellent on the history of the city, as you would expect from a native Viennese (née Pollack, she died in 1970), but very little on the Strauss family.

The life of Empress Elisabeth (Sisi) is well documented, though more in pictures than words. I have found two biographies in English, *The Reluctant Empress*, by Brigitte Hamann (Alfred A. Knopf, 1986), and *The Lonely Empress*, by Joan Haslip (Phoenix Press, 1965). Two rich books of pictures are *Empress Elisabeth of Austria 1837–1898, The Fate of a Woman Under the Yoke of the*

Imperial Court, by Renate Stephan (Austria Imperial Edition, 1998), and *Sissi, The Tragic Empress*, by Ludwig Merkle (Stiebner Verlag, 1996).

I found just a single book with any detail on the shadowy life of the emperor's mistress, Katharina Schratt. It is *The Emperor & The Actress, The Love Story of Emperor Franz Josef & Katharina Schratt,* by the empress's biographer Joan Haslip (George Weidenfeld & Nicolson, 1982), and I have used it extensively in my account of the relationship.

Particularly good on the difficult, and tragic, life of Crown Prince Rudolf is *A Nervous Splendor, Vienna 1888–1889,* by Frederic Morton (Little, Brown, 1979), a narrow account of two turbulent years in Vienna, written by a native-born Viennese now resident in the United States.

Finally two (to me) priceless little picture books that I found in Vienna many years ago, each stocked full of photographs of the old city, many of which I have reproduced in this book. They are *Wien, Innere Stadt 1850–1860* (Verlag für Photographie, 1995), and *Das Wiener Kaffeehaus 1870–1930* (H. Seemann und Chr. Lunzer, 2000).

If a picture is worth a thousand words, this is a very long book indeed.

Acknowledgements

As with my previous book *Beethoven: The Man Revealed*, it was Darren Henley, then Managing Director of Classic FM, who commissioned me to write the story of the Strauss dynasty and the city of Vienna in which father and sons lived. My gratitude to him is boundless, and I wish him every success in his new role as Chief Executive of Arts Council, England.

Once again, I am grateful to Lorne Forsyth, Chairman of Elliott & Thompson, Classic FM's publisher, for his support throughout, and to my editor Olivia Bays, Director at Elliott & Thompson. Olivia is a superb editor and a joy to work with. I set Pippa Crane, Senior Editor at Elliott & Thompson, a Herculean task in tracking down the best part of a hundred illustrations and the book is infinitely better for her efforts.

The eagle eyes of copyeditor Jill Burrows corrected several inconsistencies in the manuscript and improved some infelicities of style, and James Collins designed a book that far outshone my expectations, as he did with *Beethoven*.

To see the two books side by side on my shelf, I confess rather immodestly, causes me some pride.

About Classic FM

Classic FM is the biggest single commercial radio station and the most popular classical music brand in the UK, reaching 5.4 million listeners every week.

Classic FM's programmes are hosted by a mix of classical music experts and household names who are passionate about the genre including John Suchet, Alexander Armstrong, Myleene Klass, Bill Turnbull, Alan Titchmarsh, Aled Jones, Margherita Taylor, Alex James, Nicholas Owen, Charlotte Green, Catherine Bott and Tim Lihoreau.

Since its launch in 1992, Classic FM has made classical music from the past millennium accessible and relevant to today's audience. The station is celebrating its 25th birthday in 2017.

Classic FM is owned by Global, the media & entertainment group.

You can tune into Classic FM across the UK on 100–102 FM, digital radio and TV, at ClassicFM.com and on the Classic FM app.

Source: RAJAR / Ipsos-MORI / RSMB, period ending December 18th 2016.

Index

About the Author

John Suchet presents Classic FM's flagship morning programme, from 9 a.m. every weekday. His informative style of presentation, coupled with a deep knowledge of classical music, has won a wide spectrum of new listeners to the station. Before turning to classical music, John was one of the UK's best-known television journalists. As a reporter for ITN he covered world events, including the Iran revolution, the Soviet invasion of Afghanistan and the Philippines revolution. He then became a newscaster, regularly presenting ITN's flagship *News at Ten*, as well as all other bulletins, over a period of nearly twenty years.

John has been honoured for both roles. In 1986 he was voted Television Journalist of the Year, in 1996 Television Newscaster of the Year, and in 2008 the Royal Television Society awarded him its highest accolade, a Lifetime Achievement Award. John has been given an honorary degree by his old university, the University of Dundee, and in 2001 the Royal Academy of Music awarded him an Honorary Fellowship in recognition of his work on Beethoven, having written six books on the composer, including the bestselling *Beethoven: The Man Revealed*.